Relax

THIS BOOK BELONGS TO:

....

....

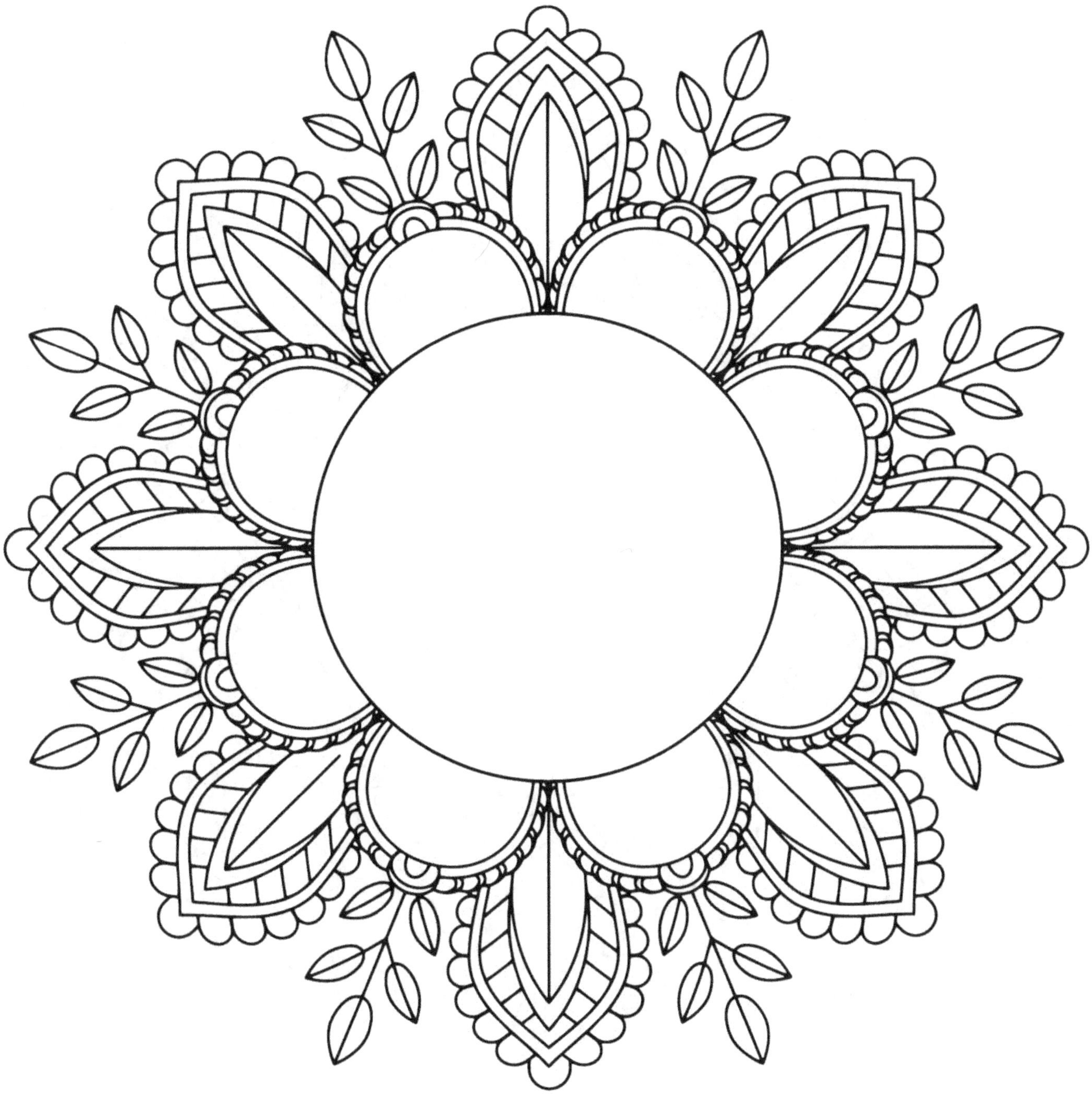

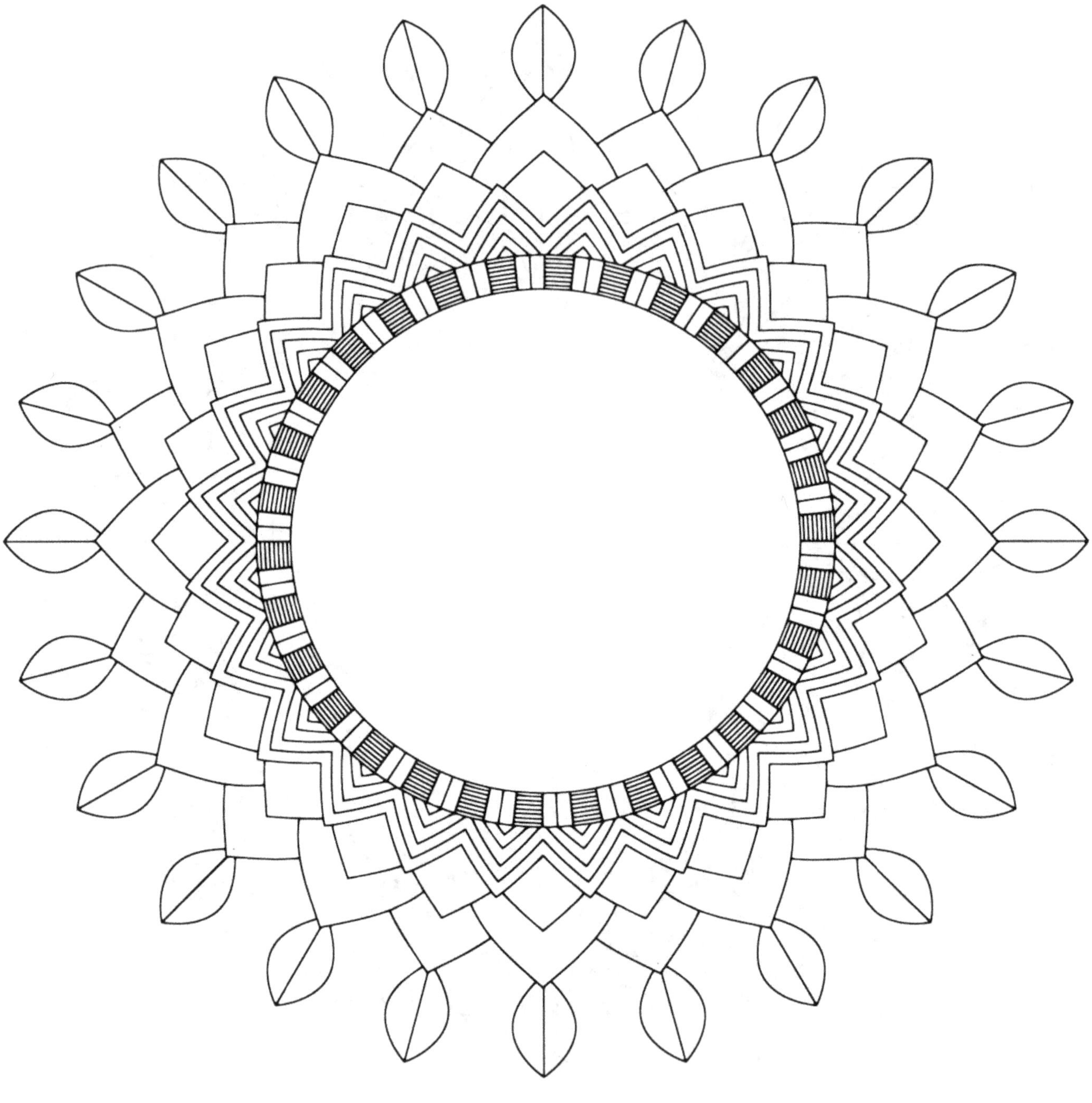

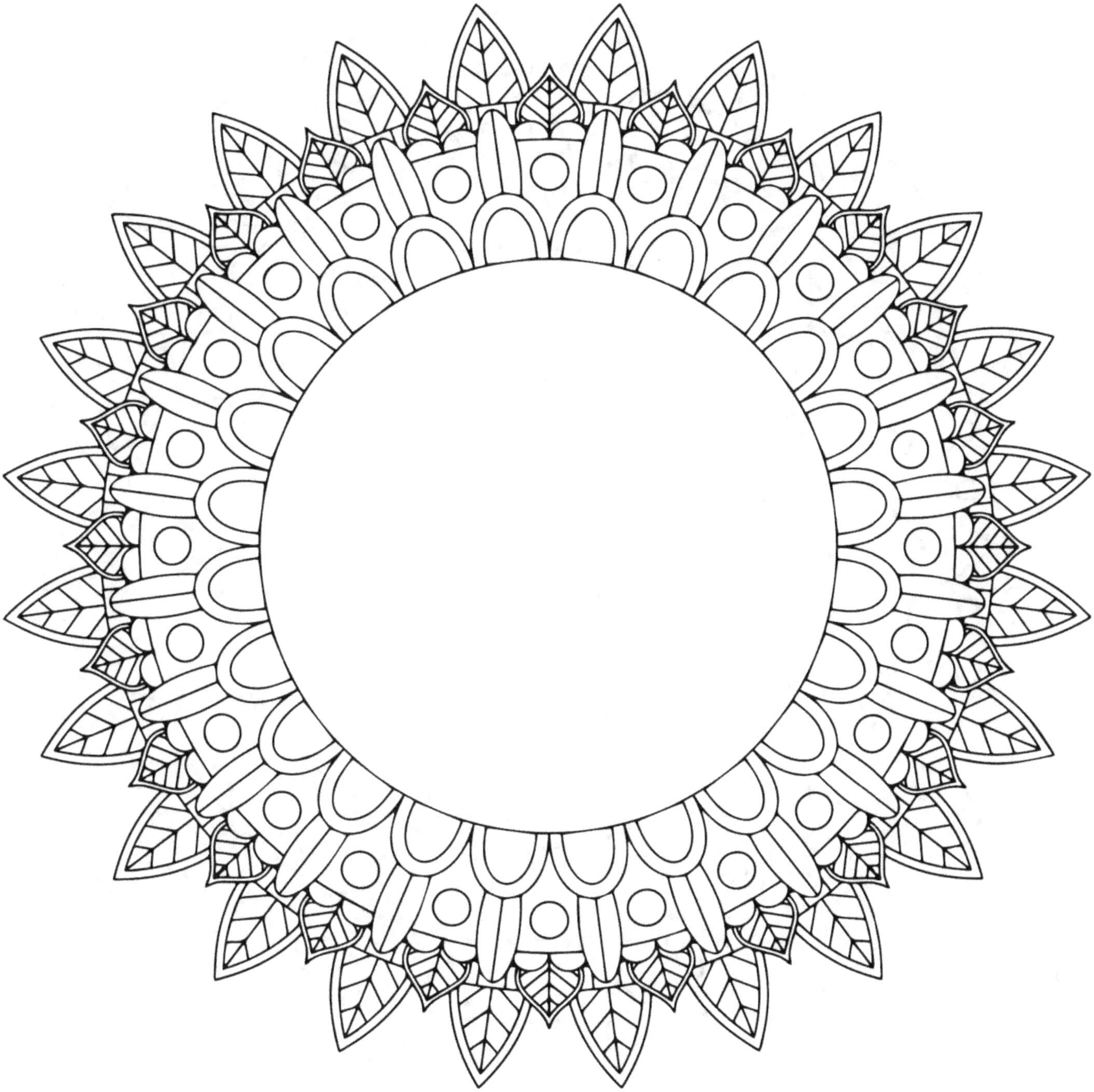

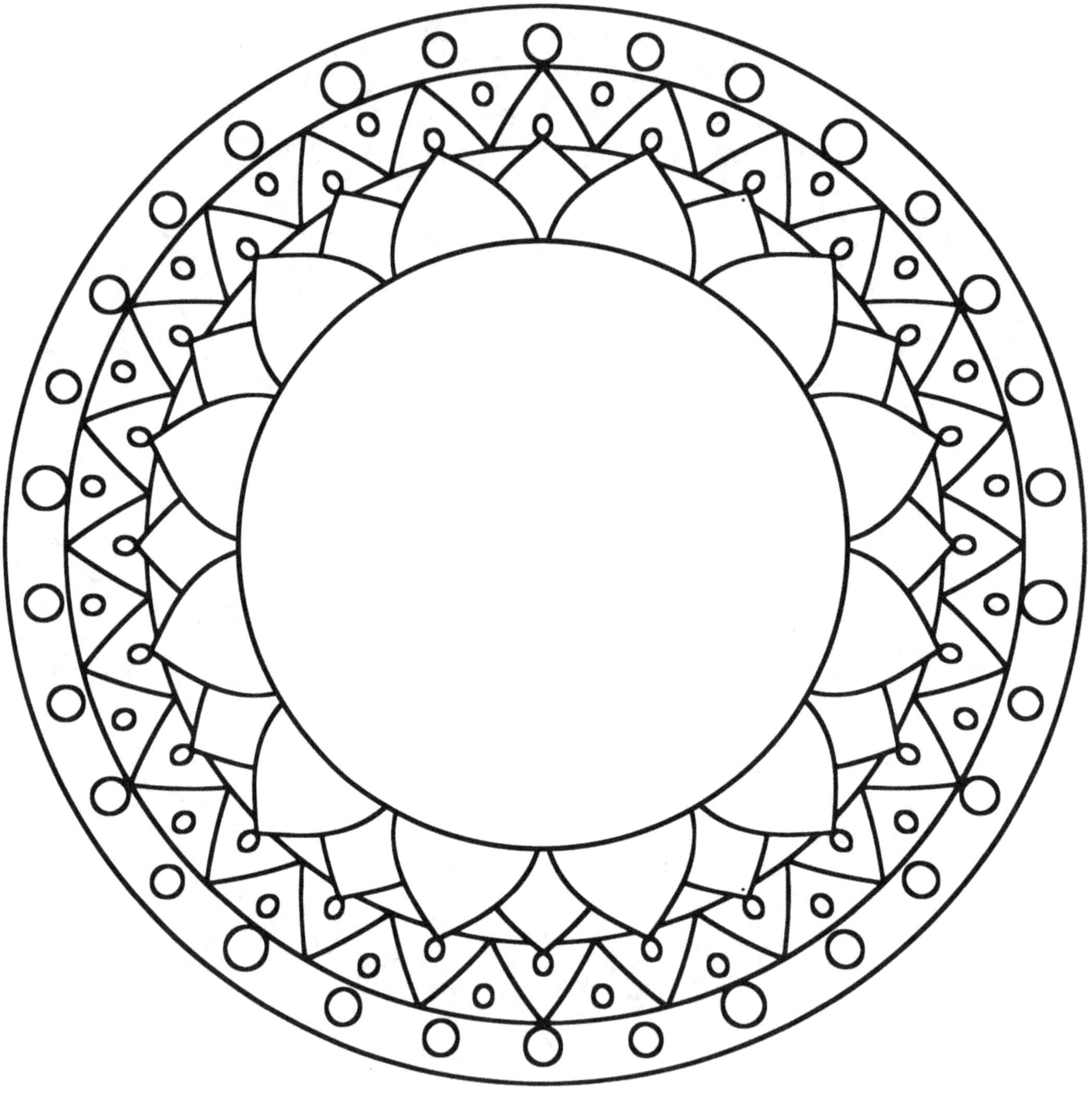

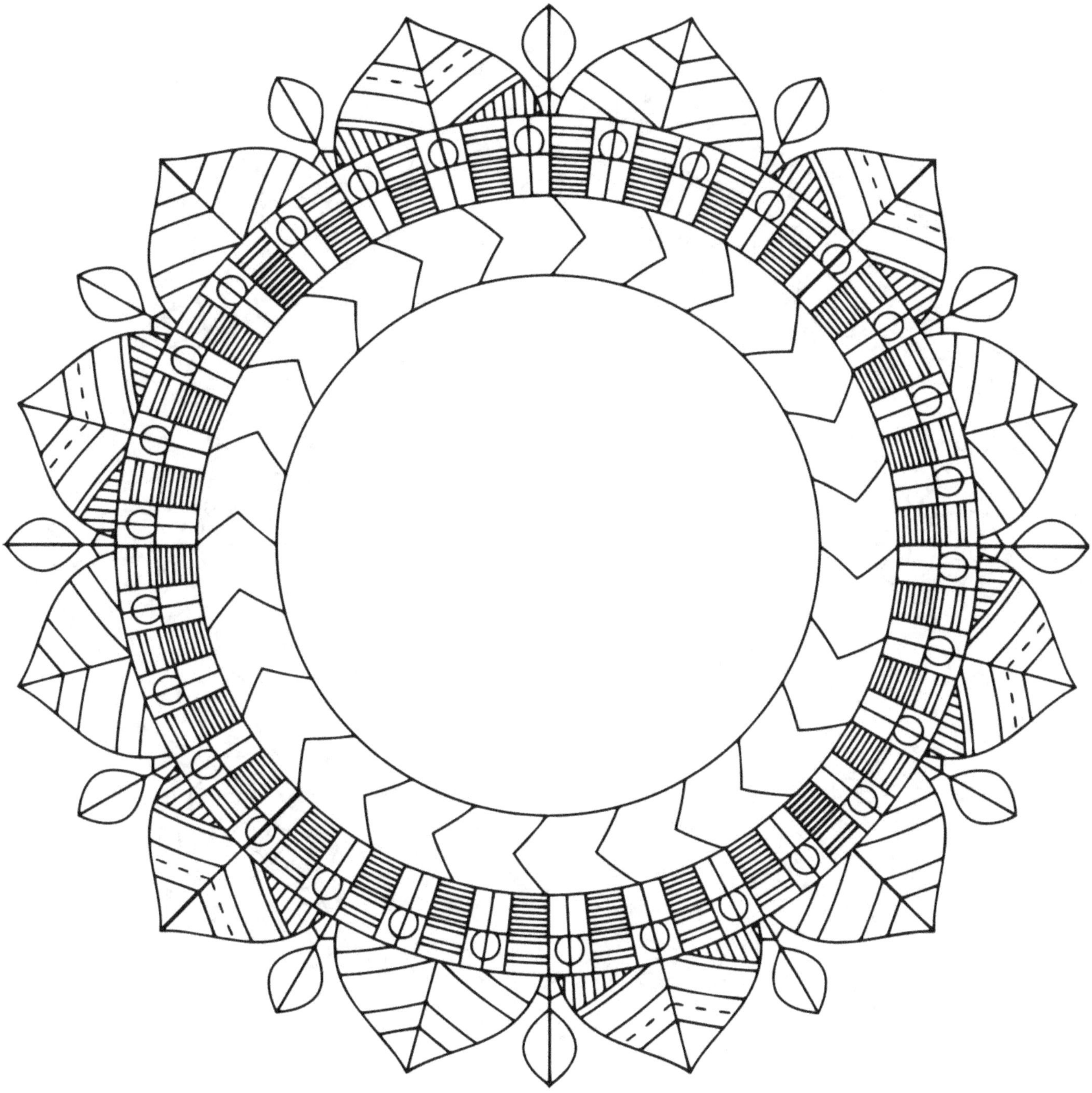

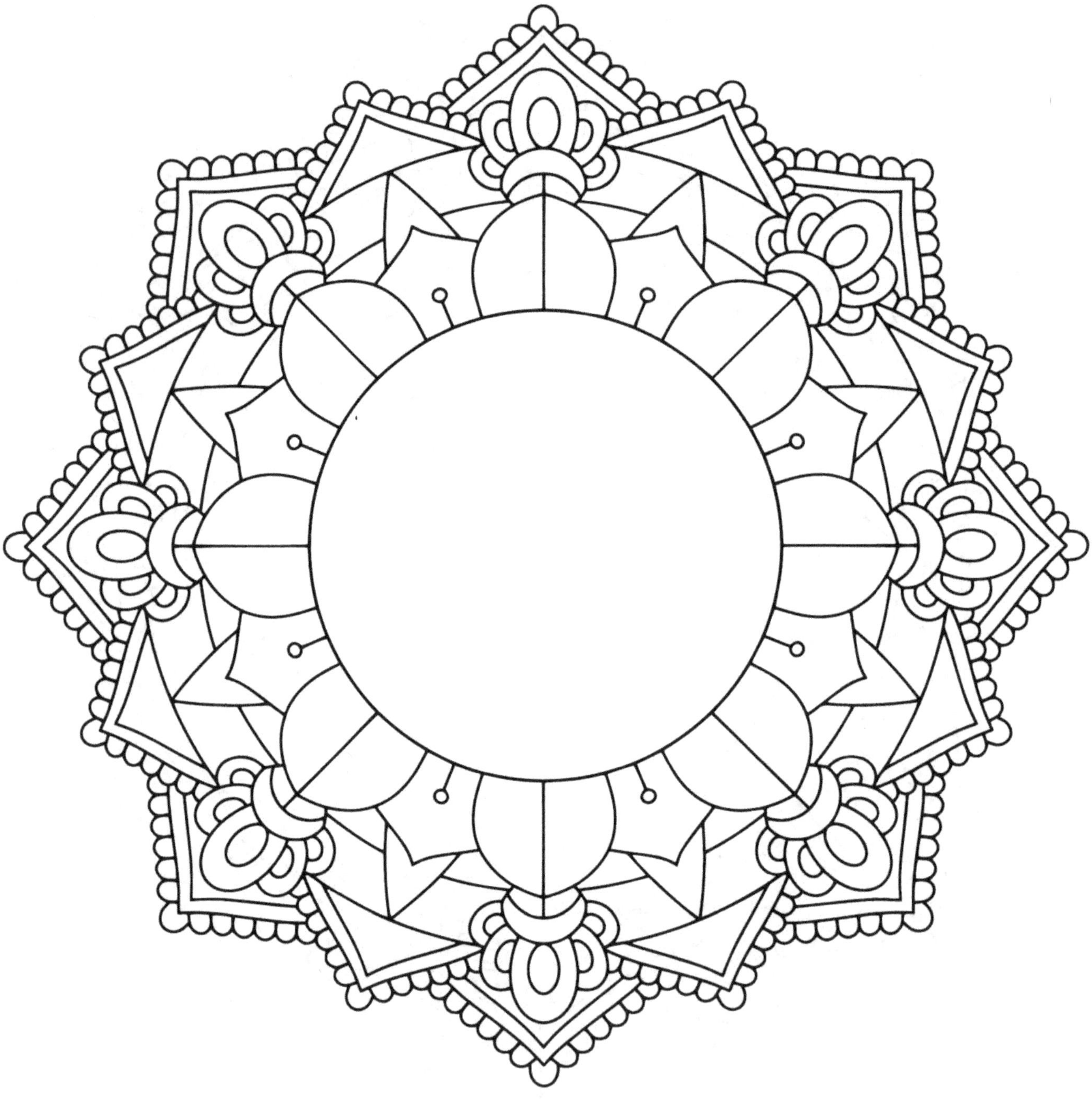

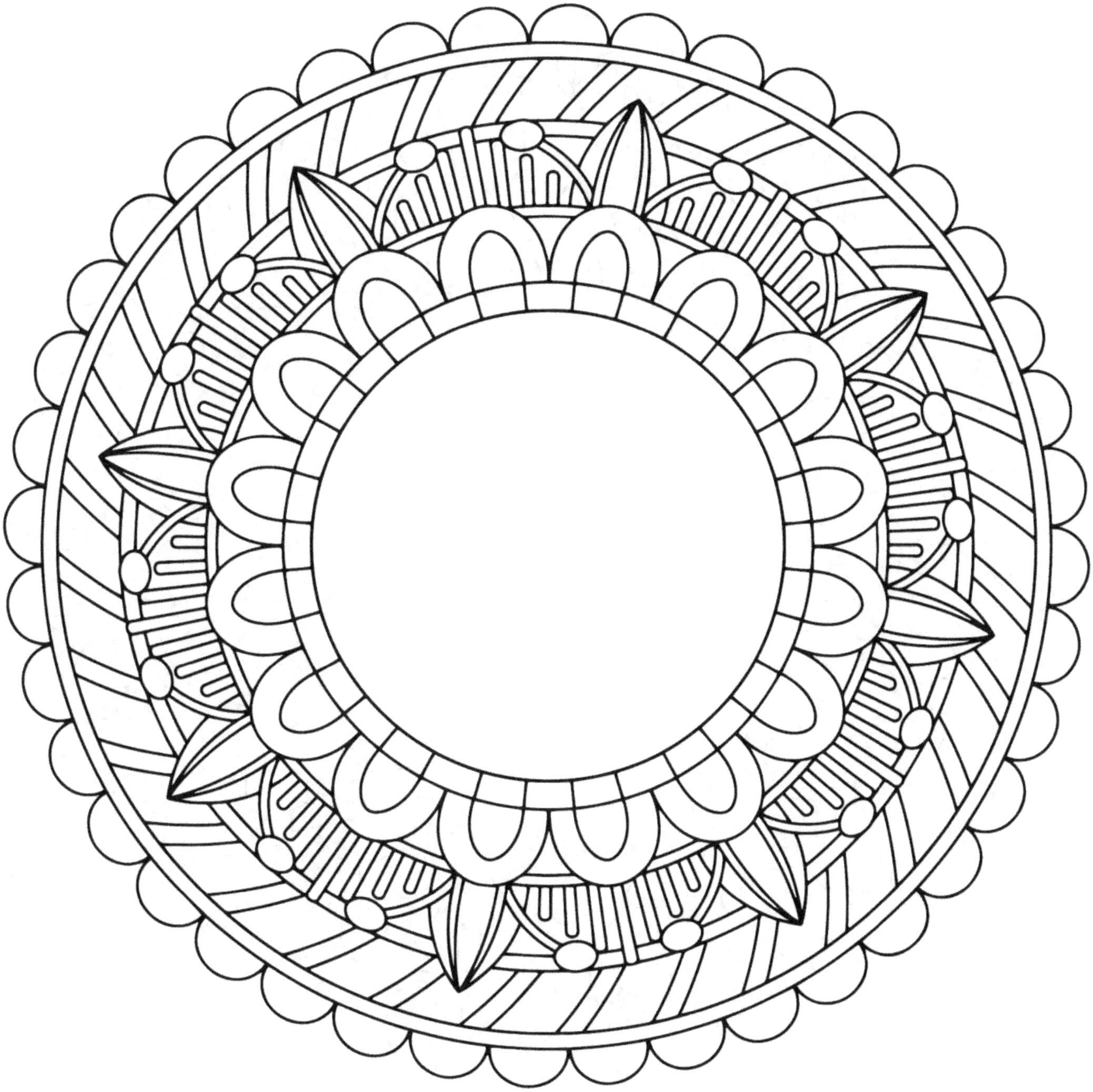

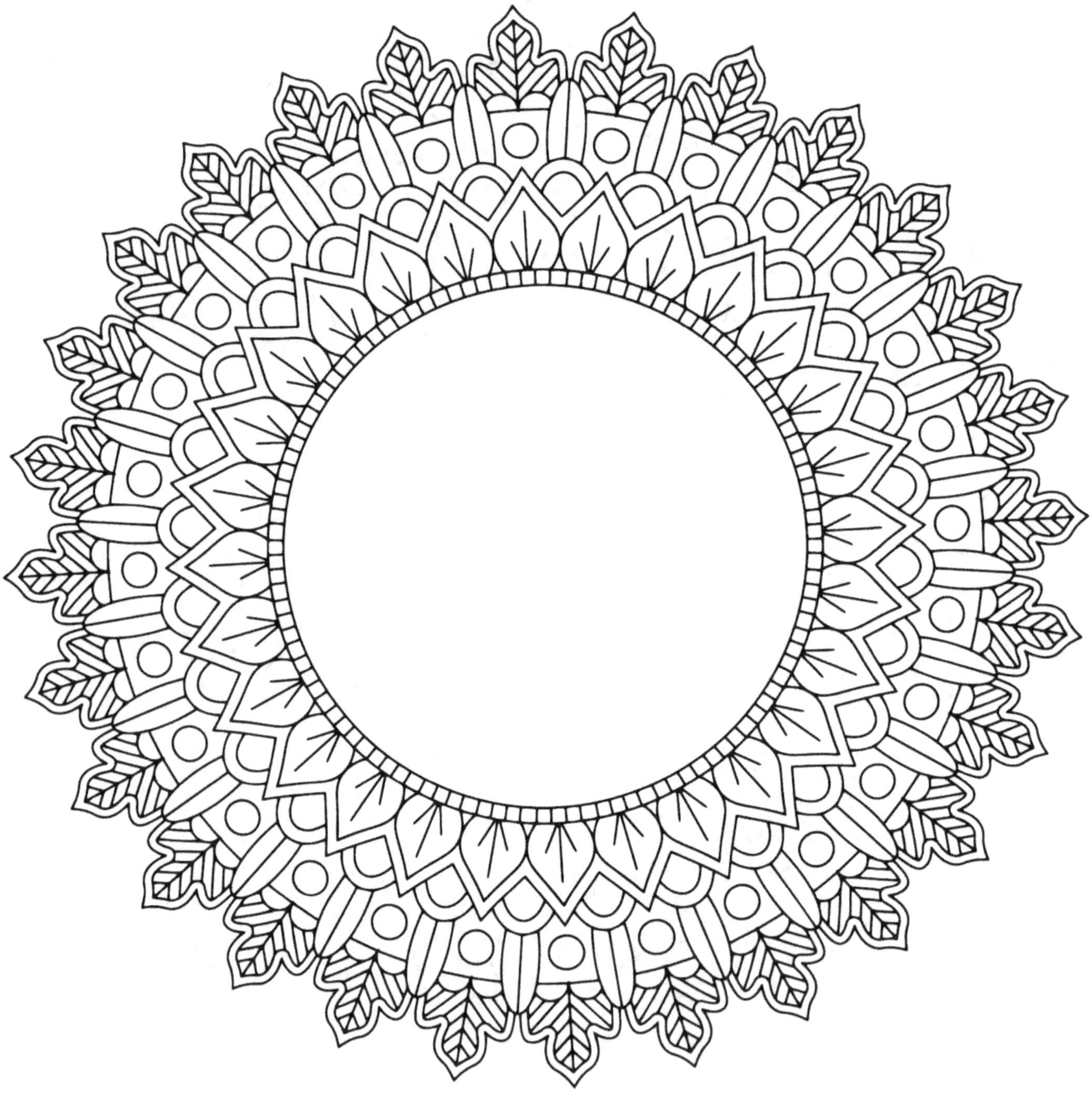

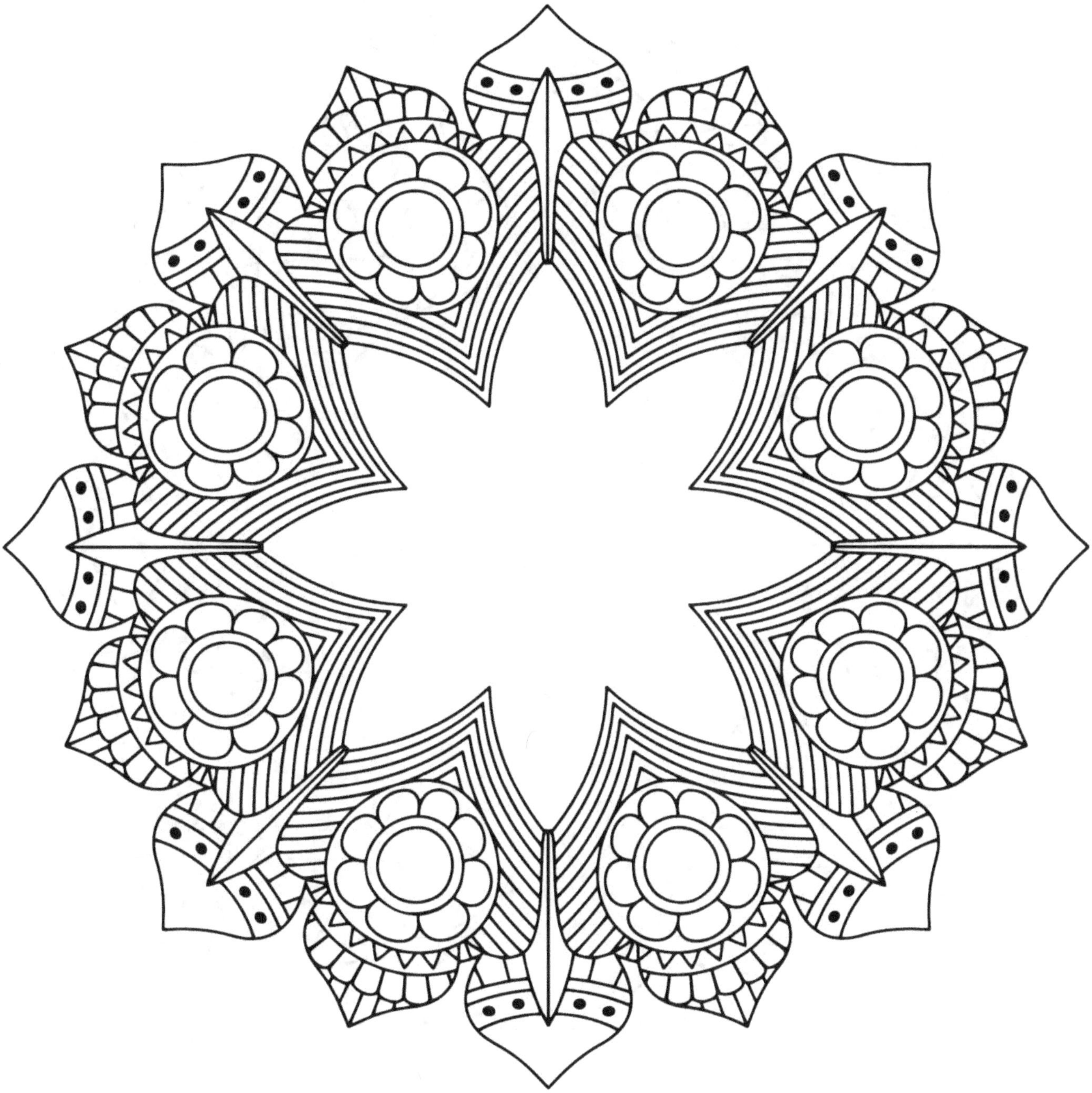

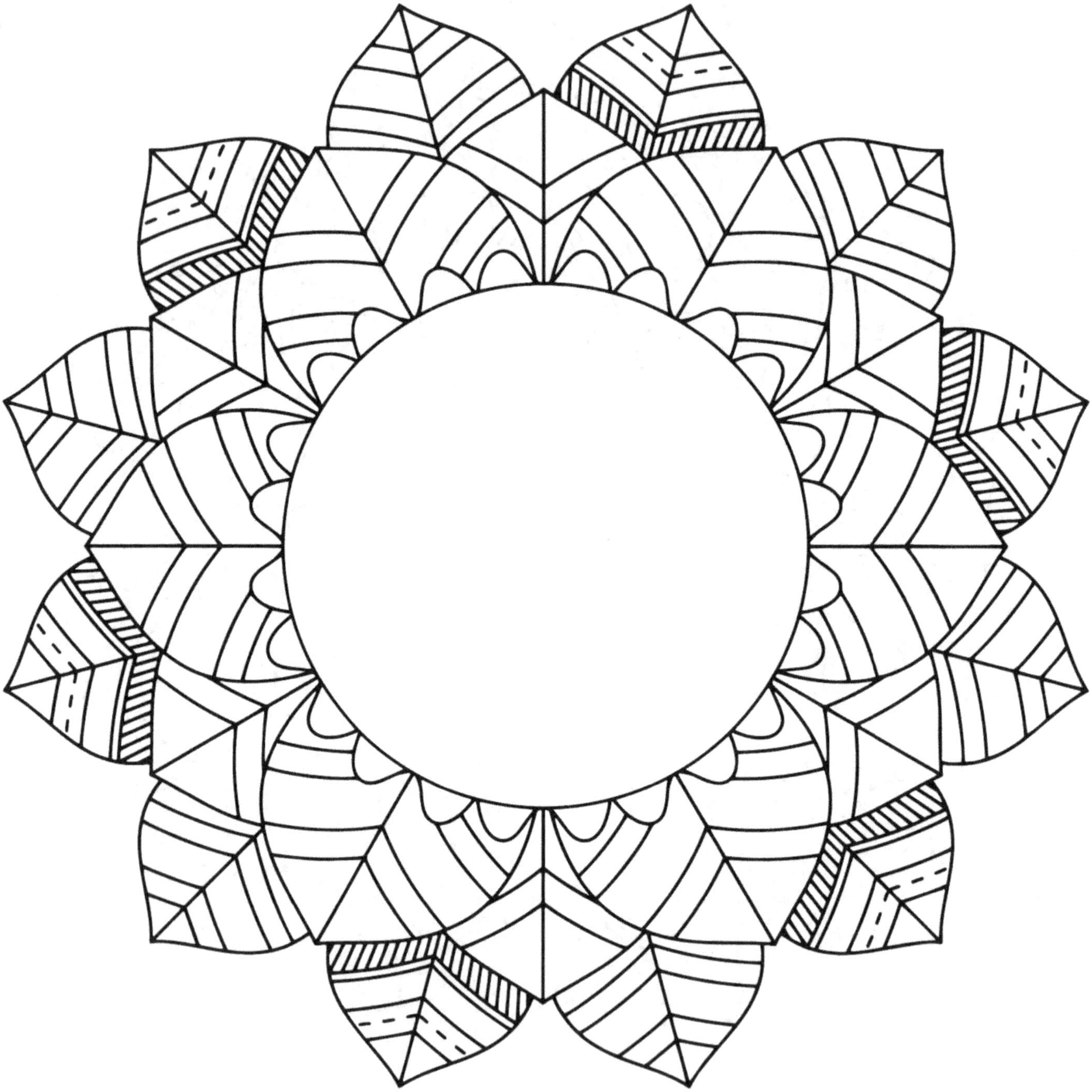

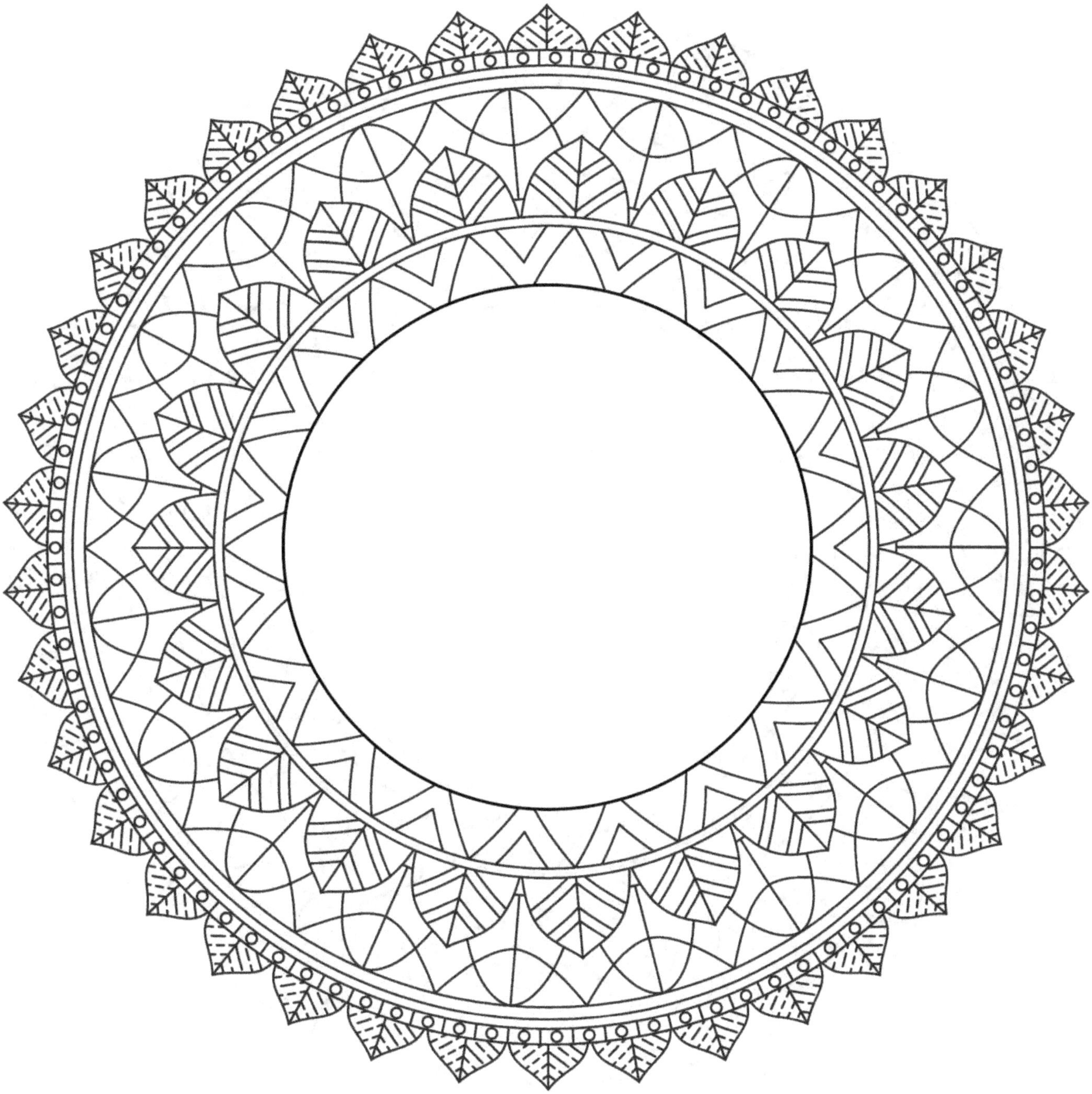

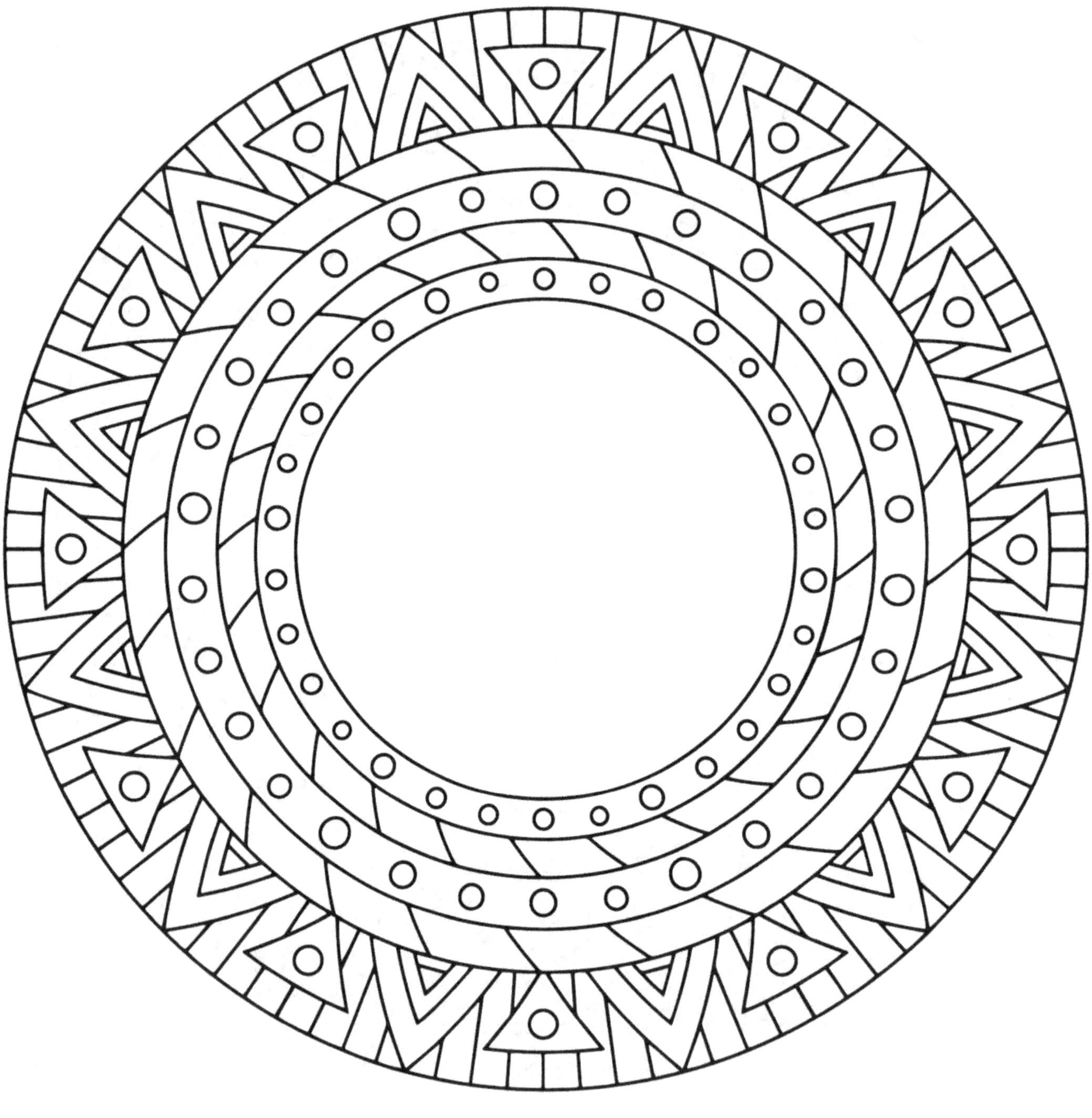

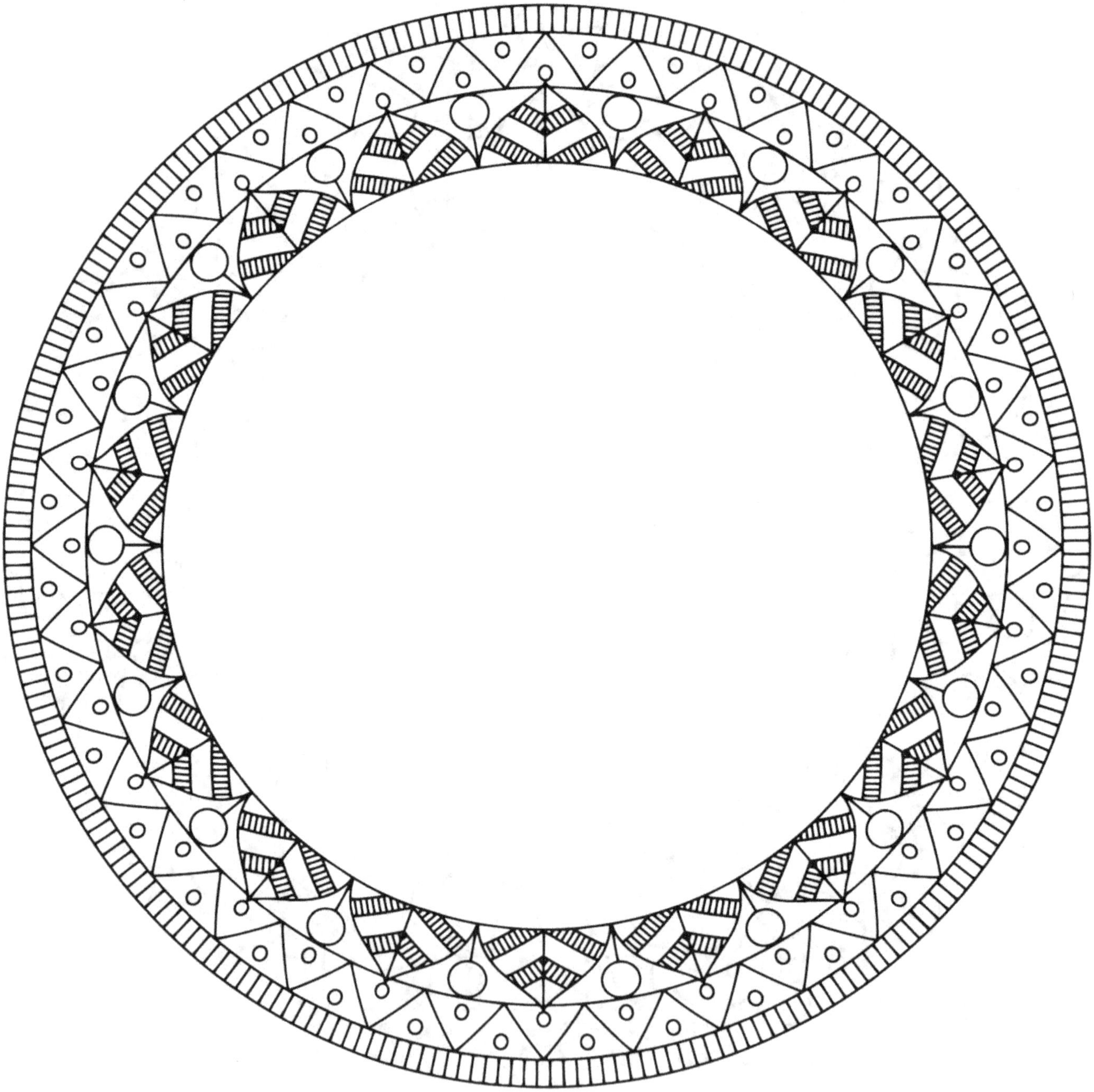

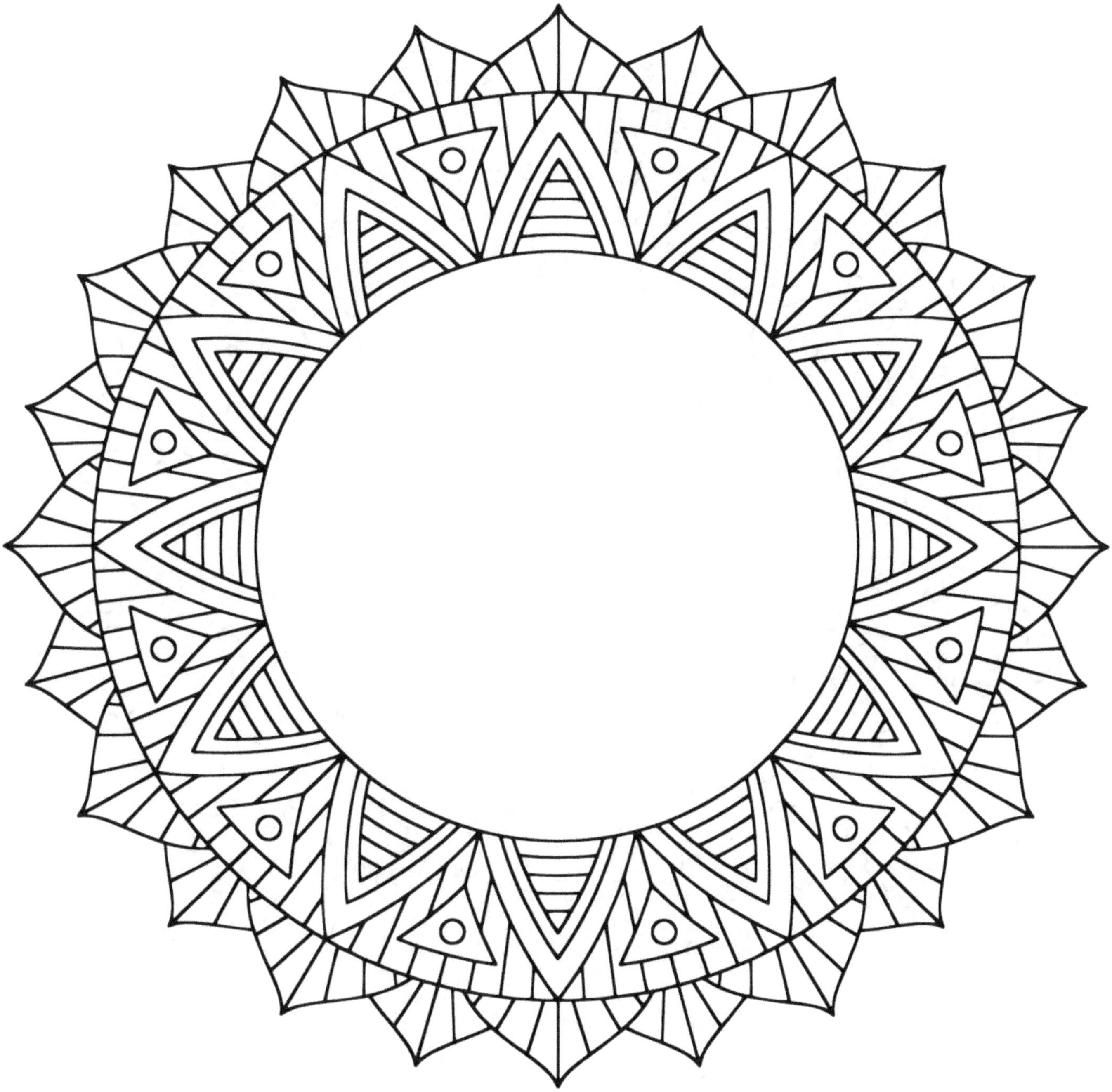

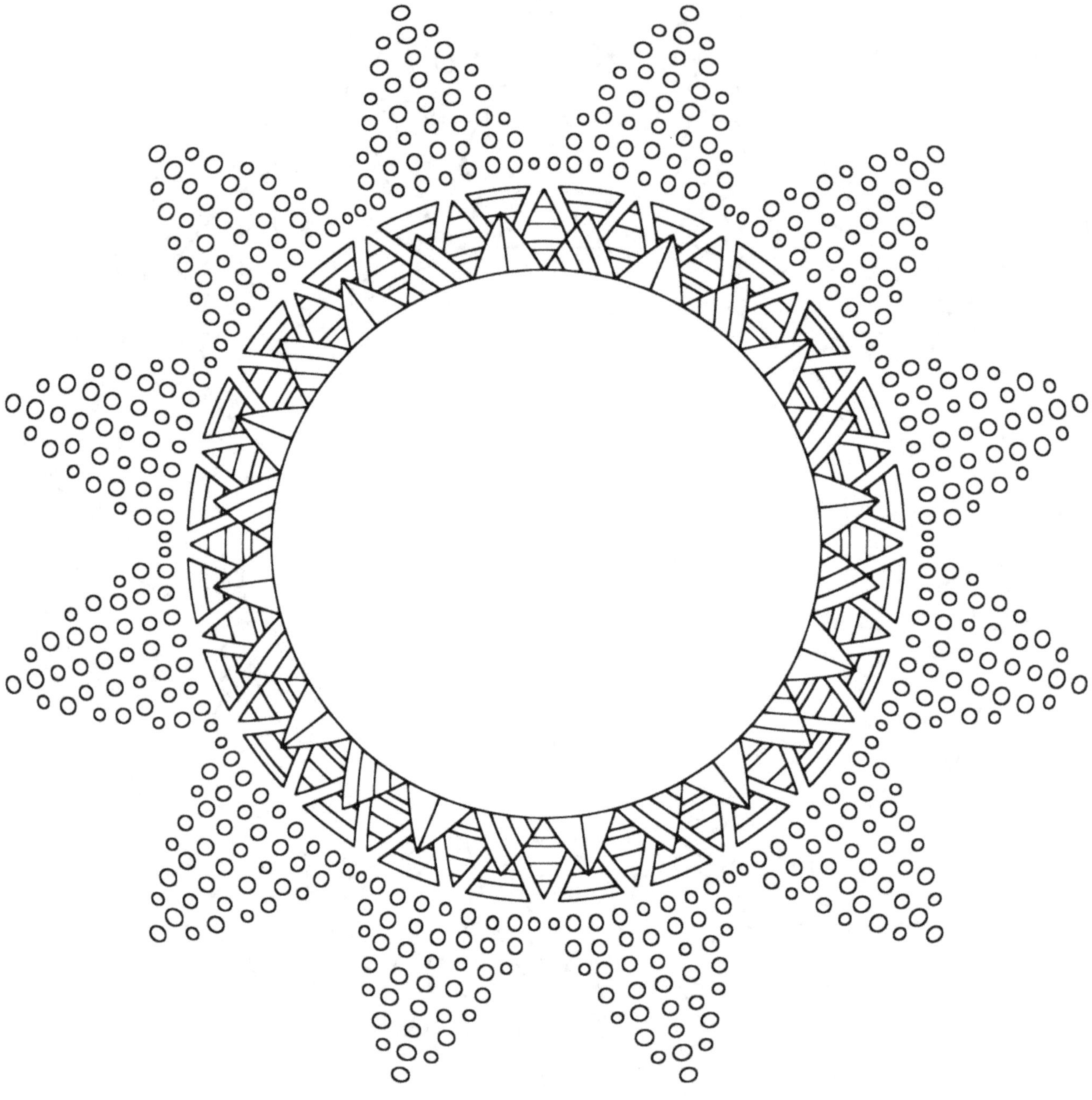

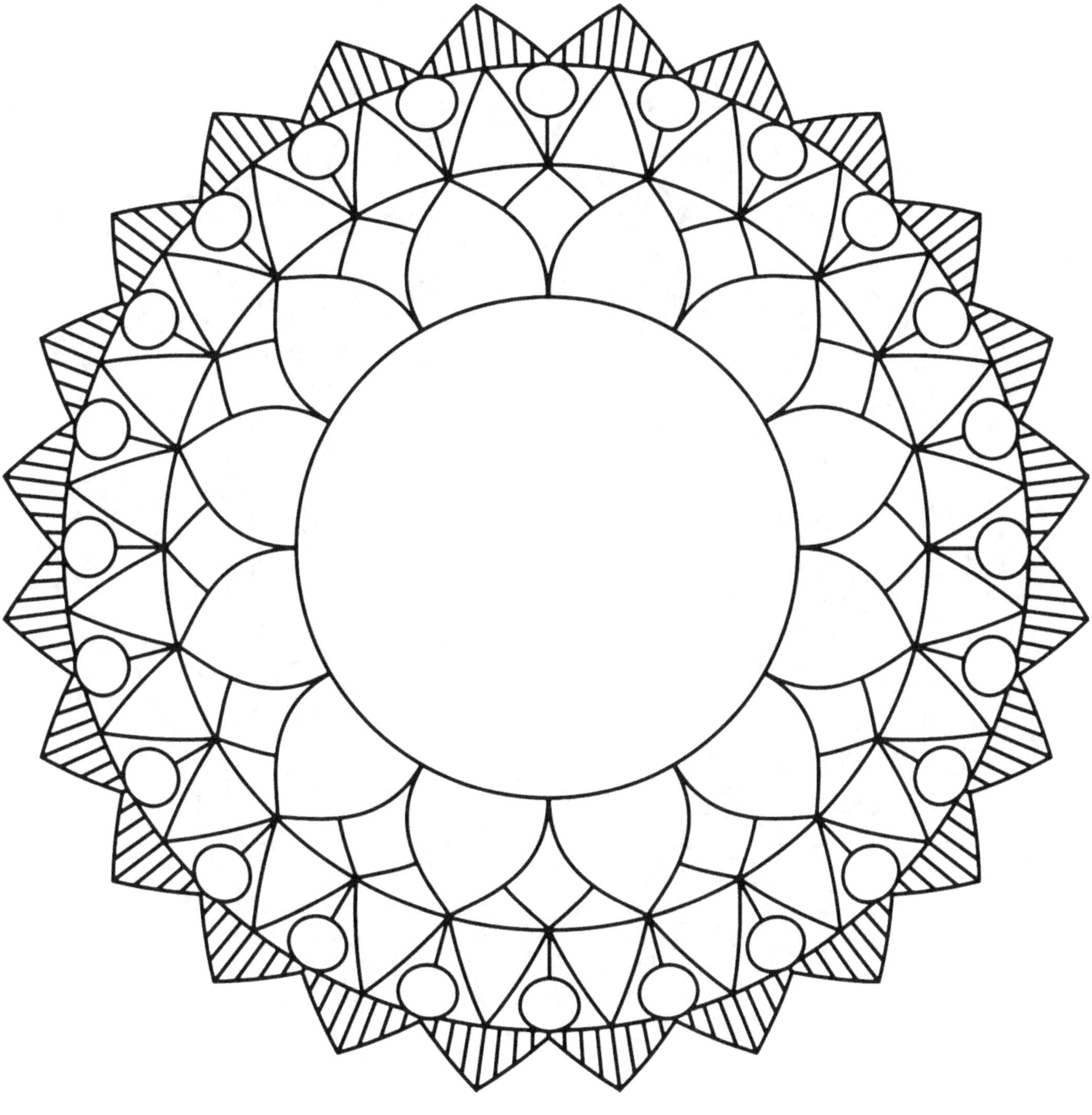

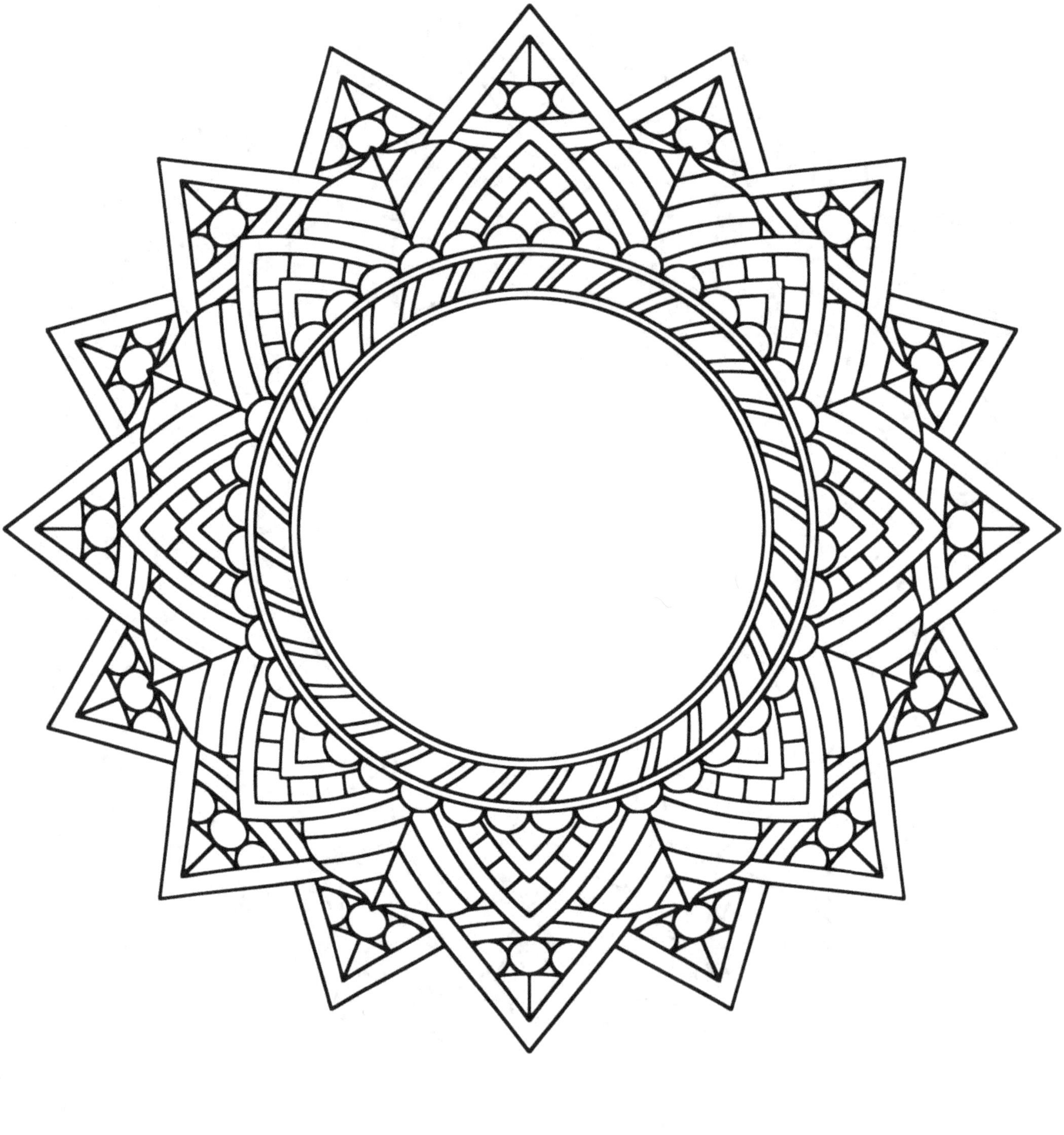

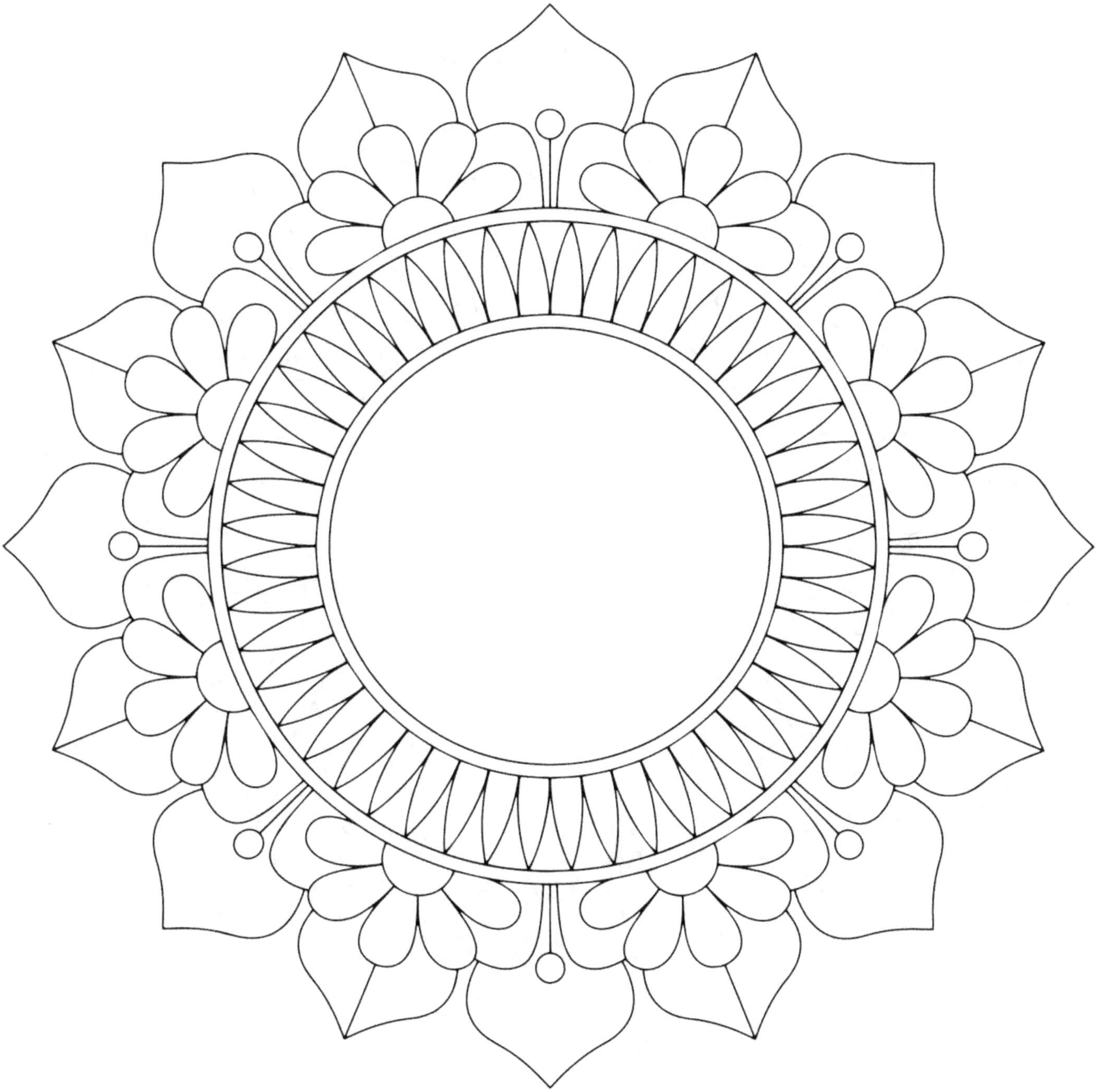

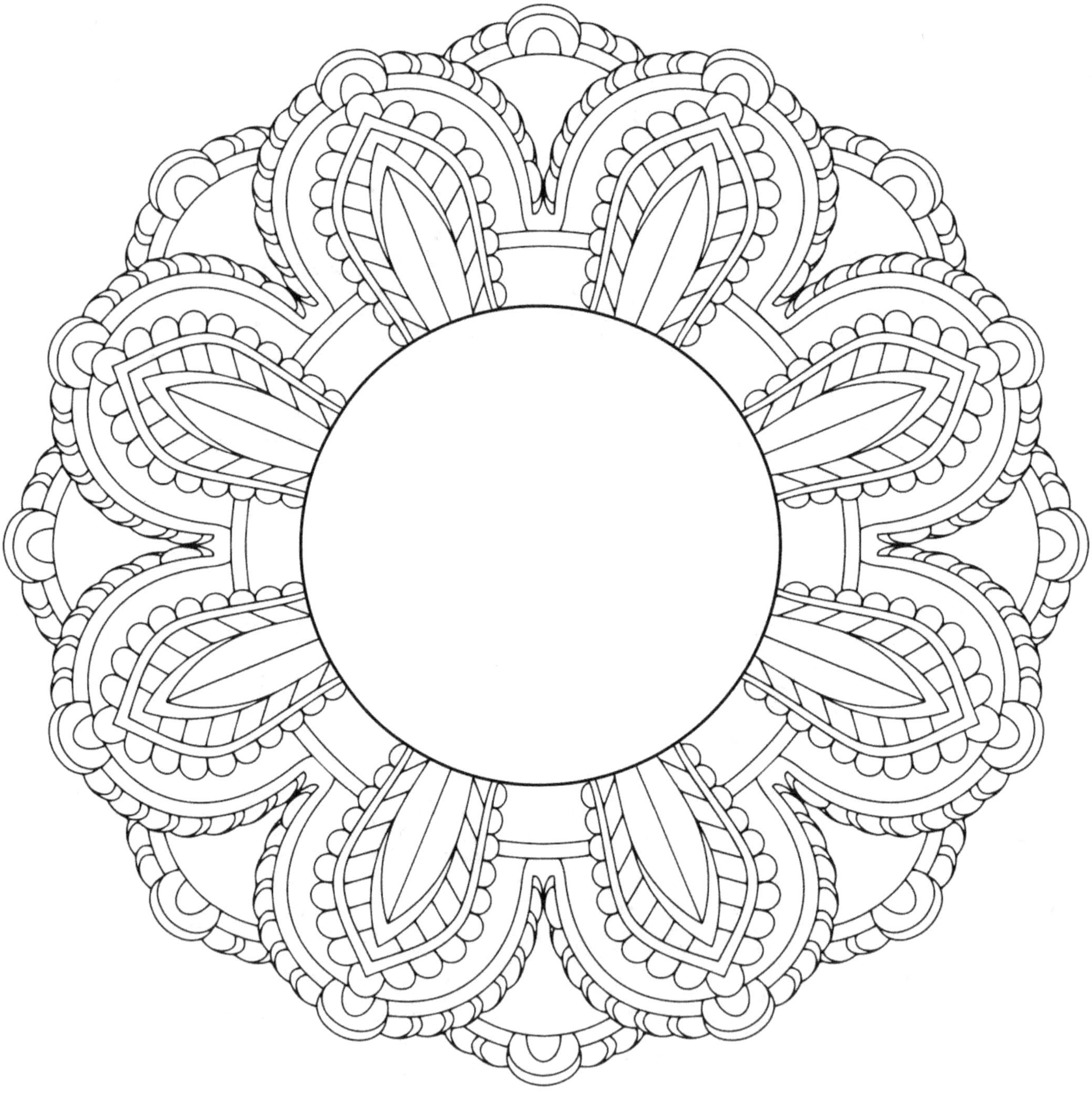

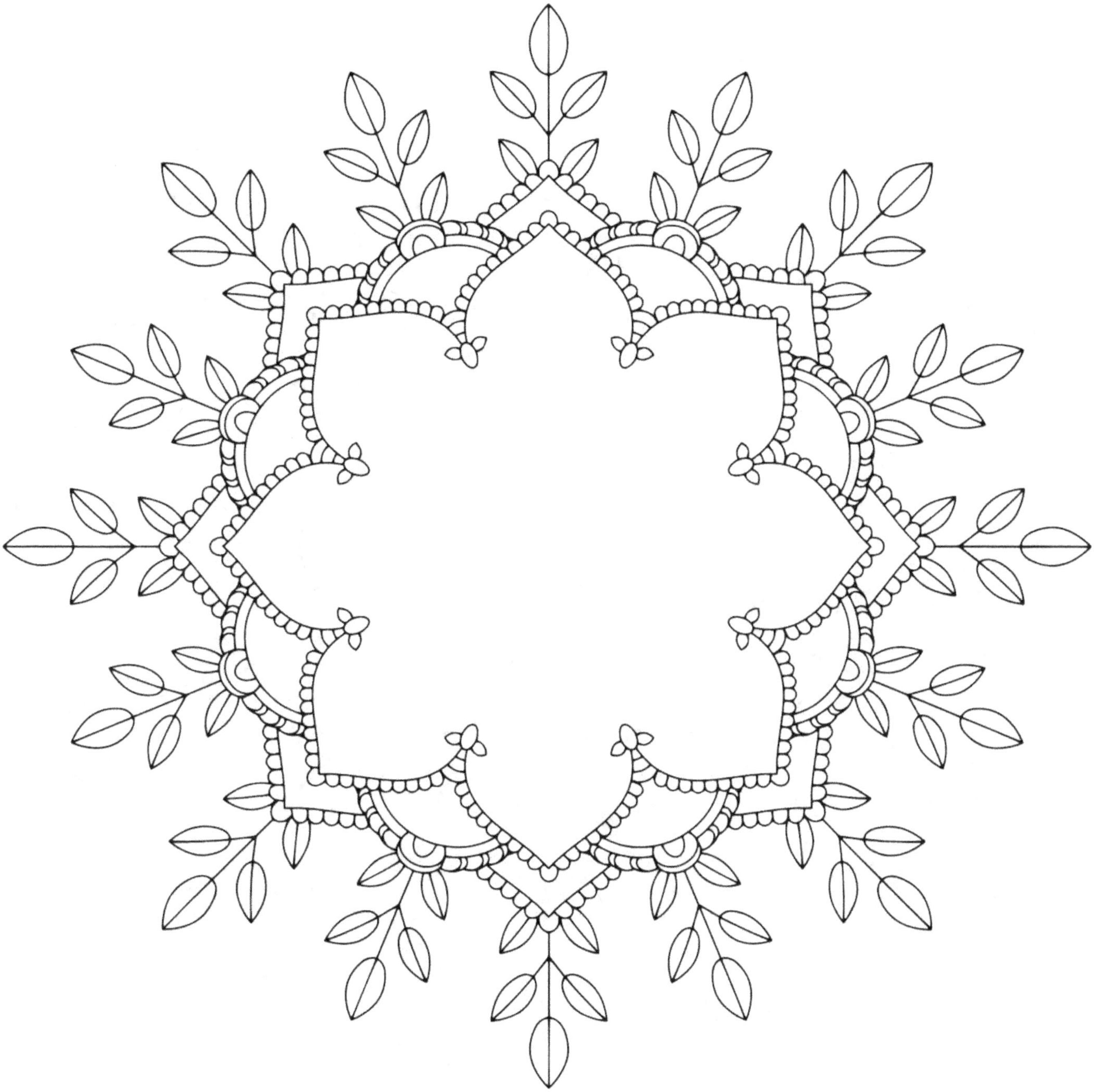

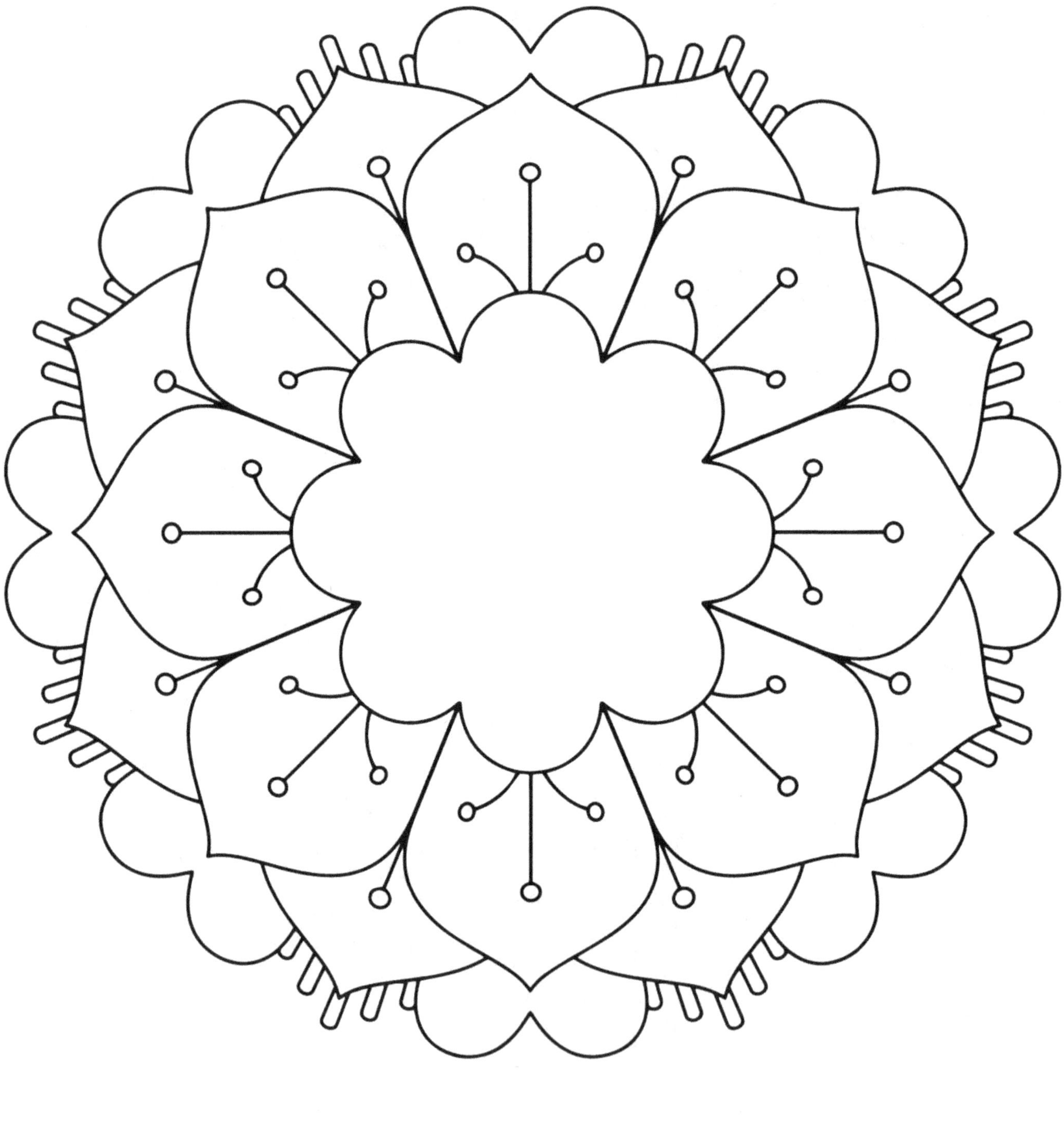

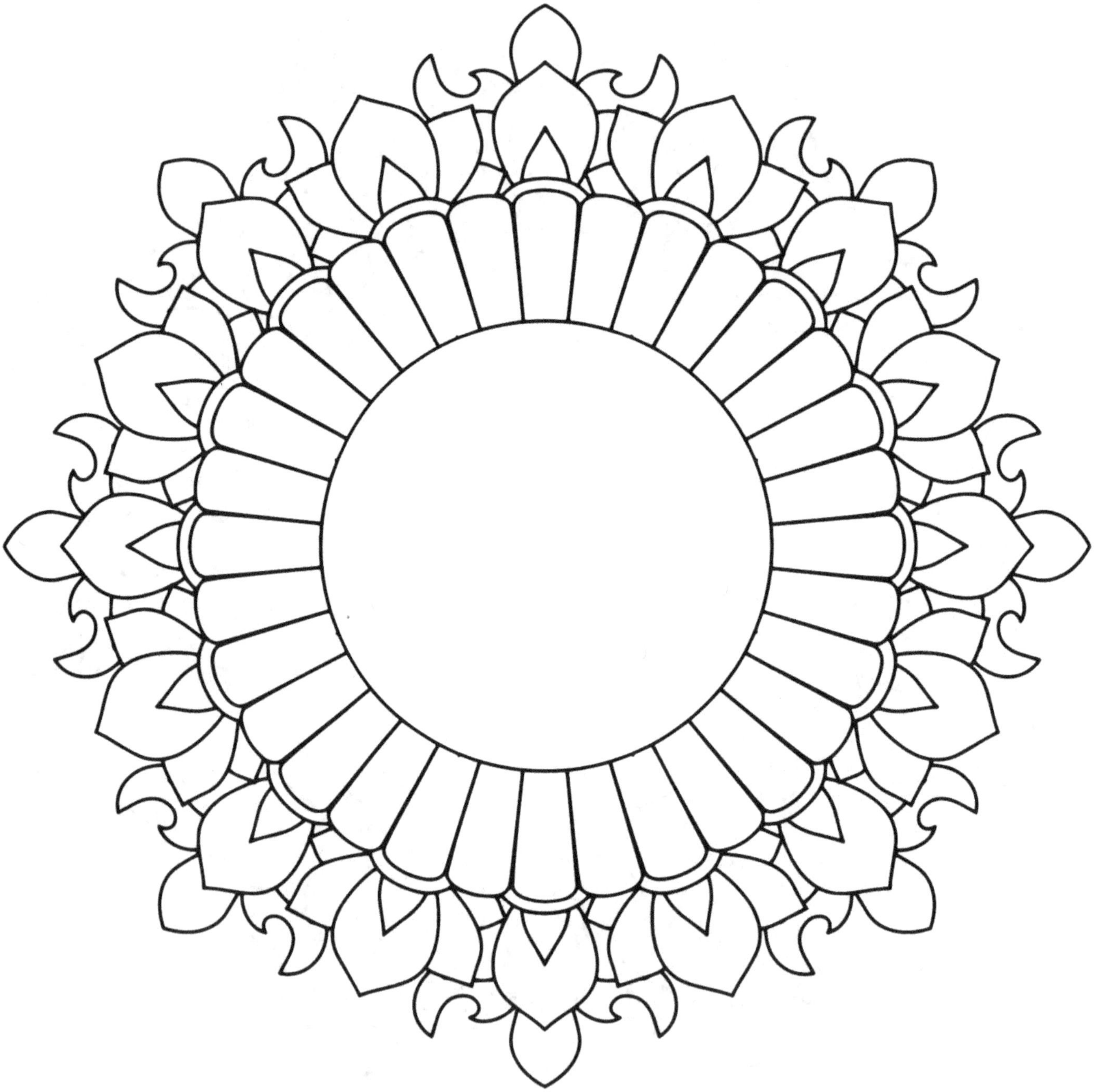

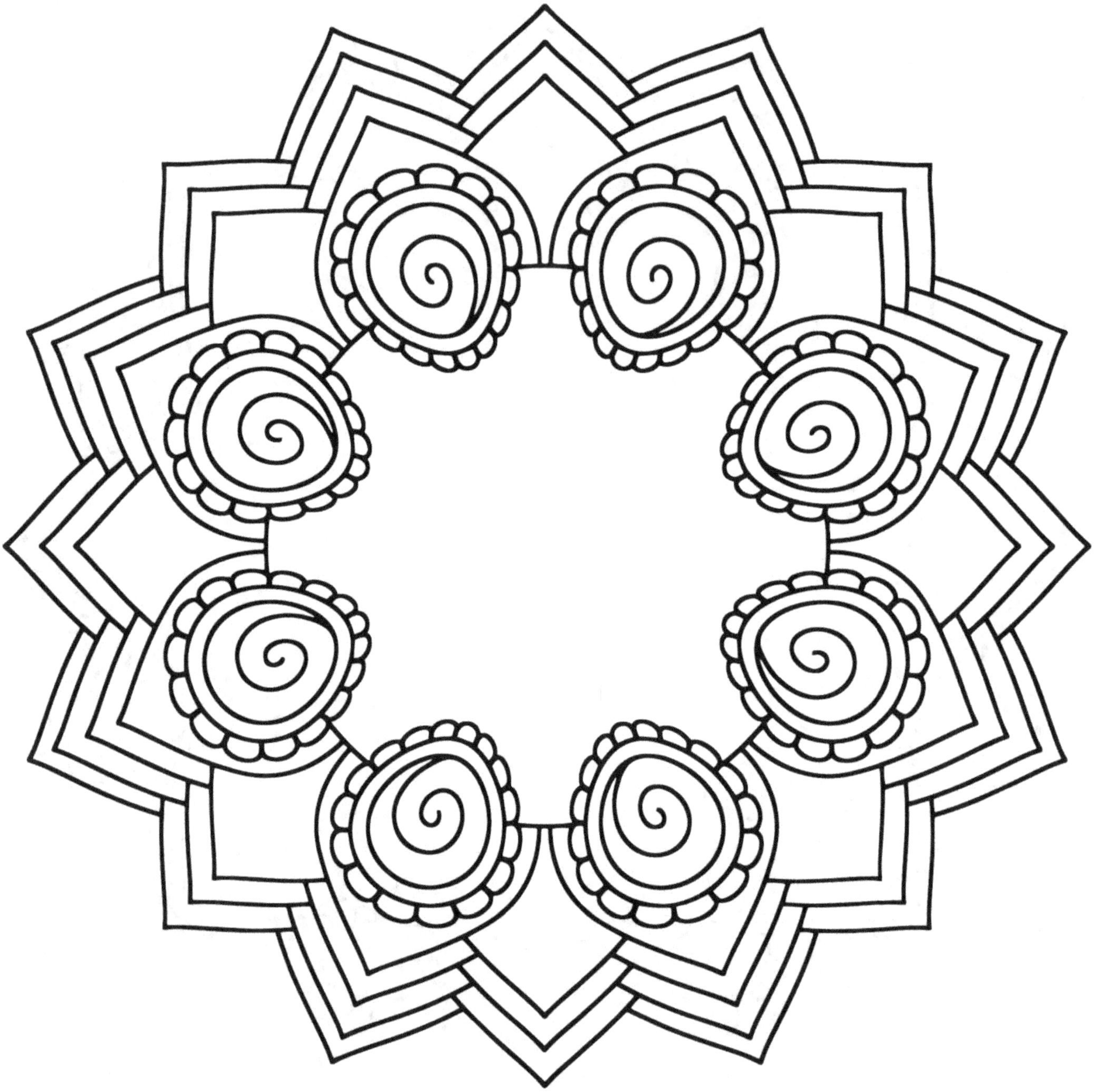

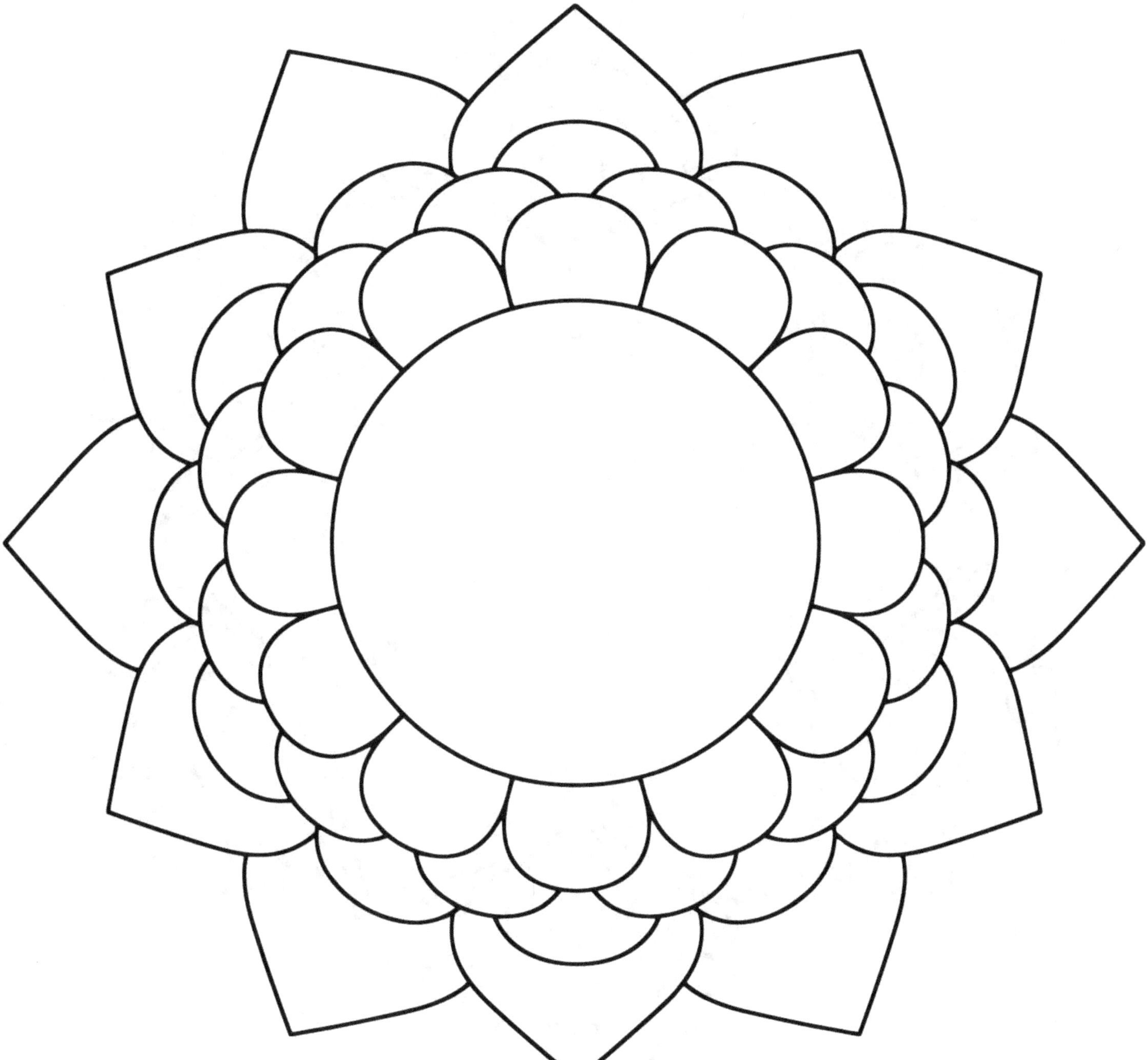

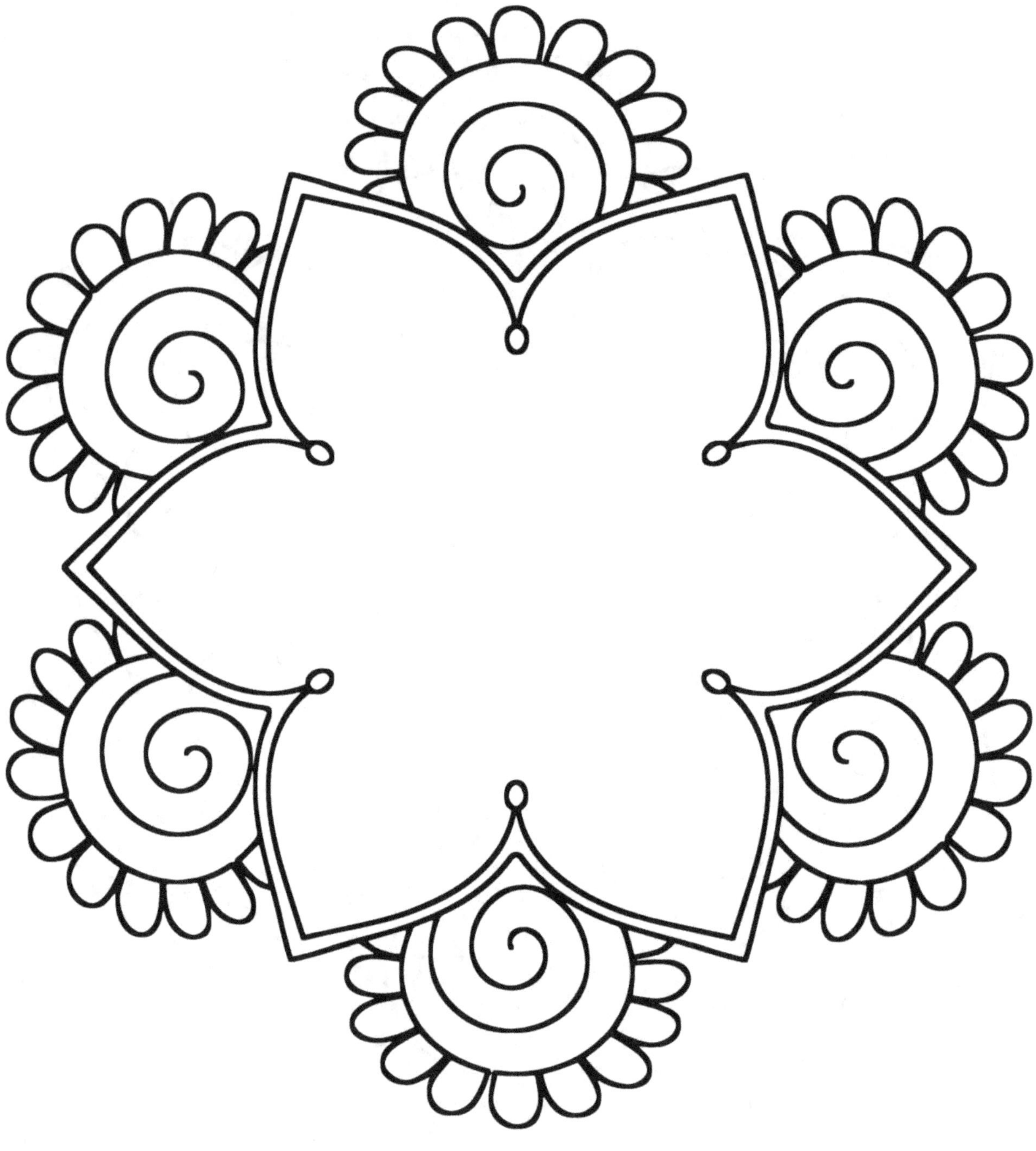

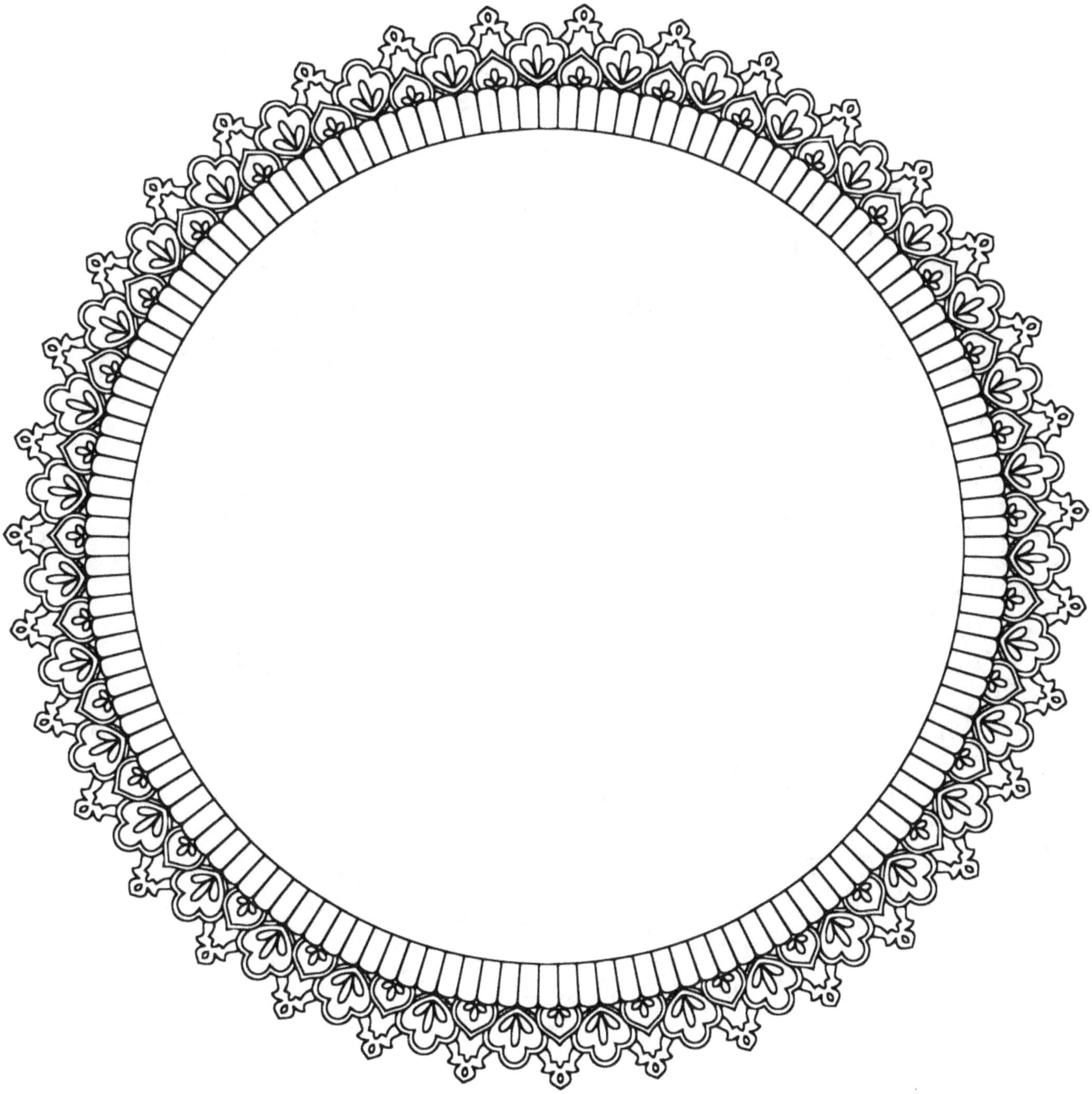

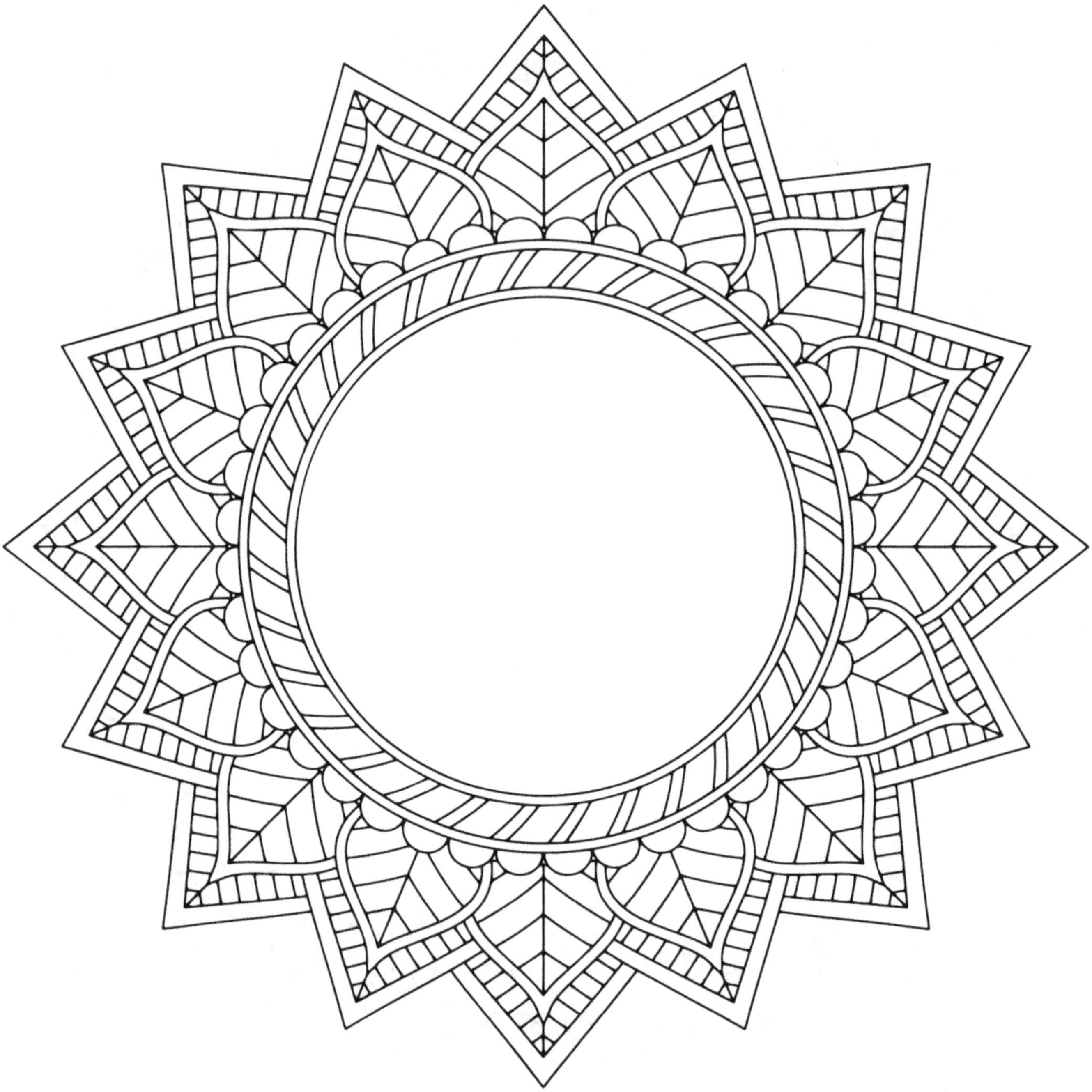

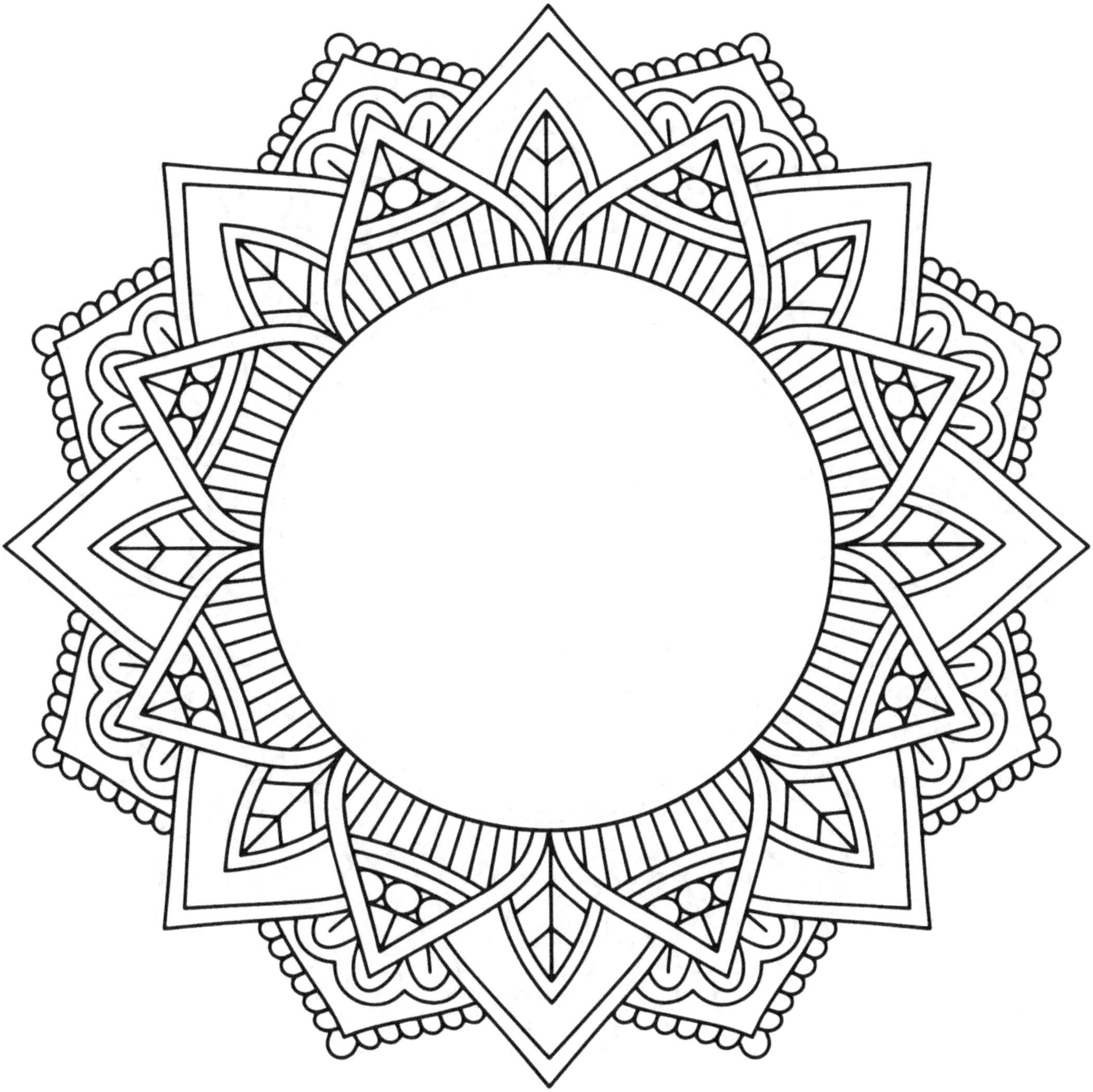

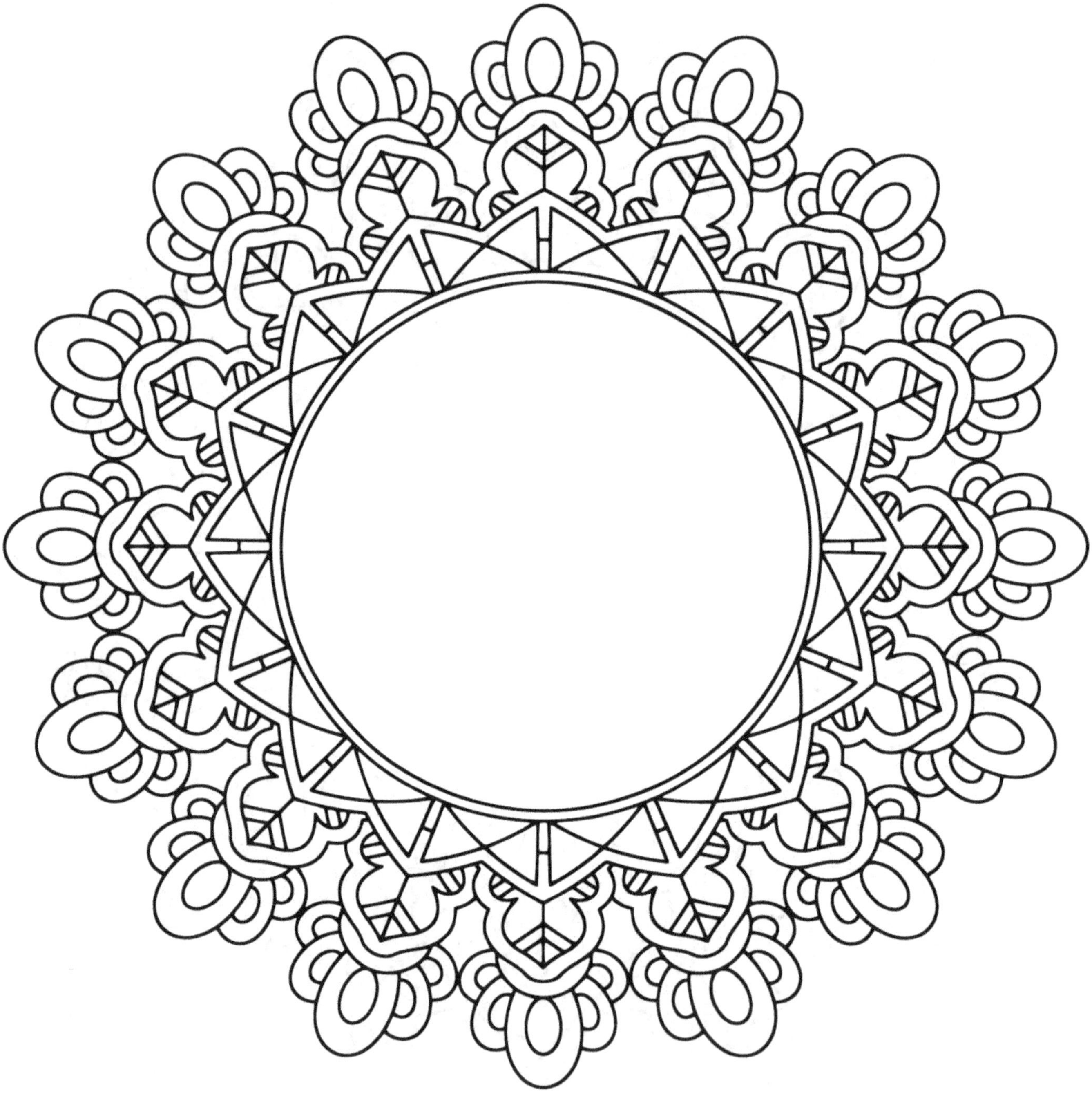

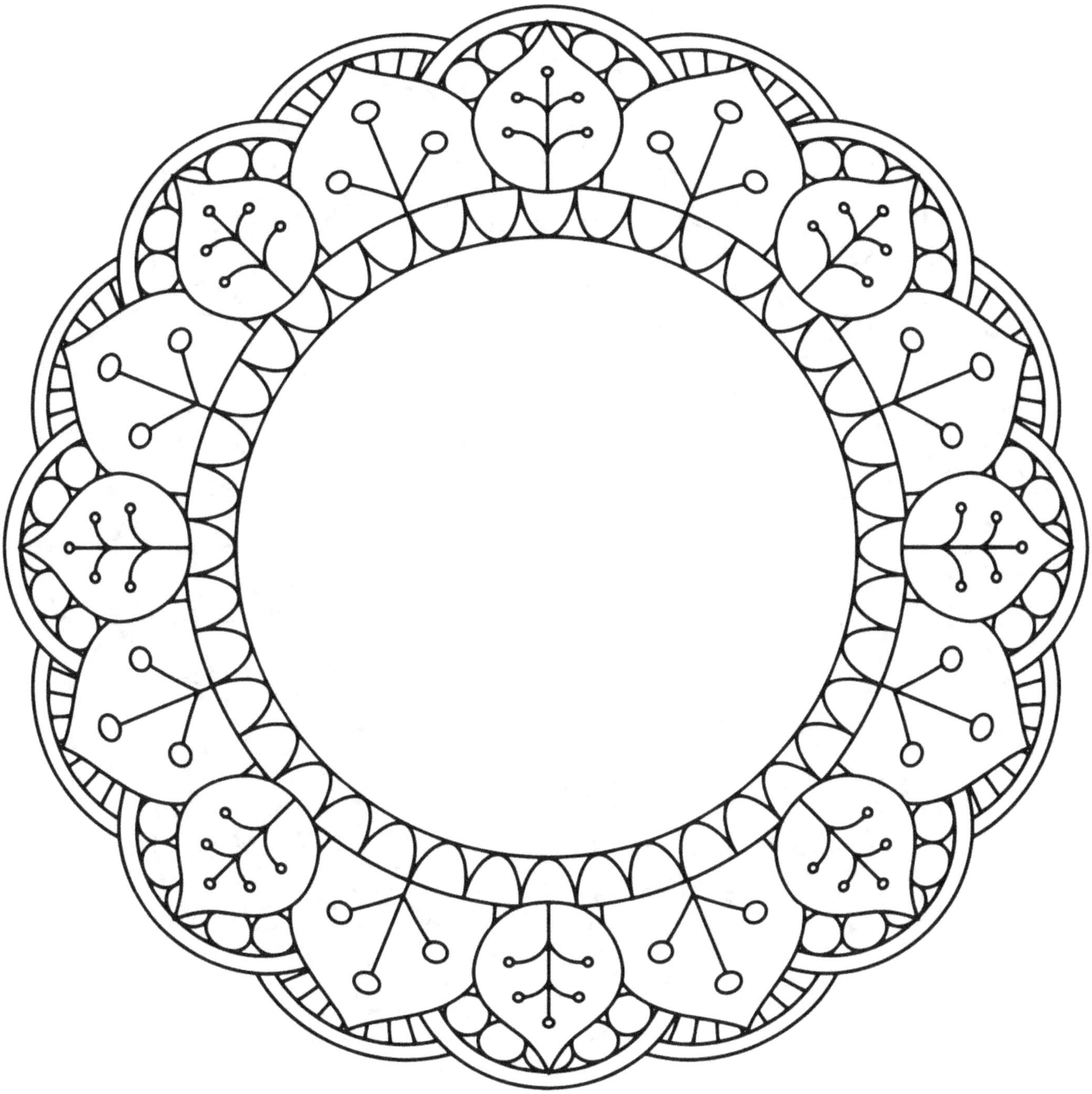

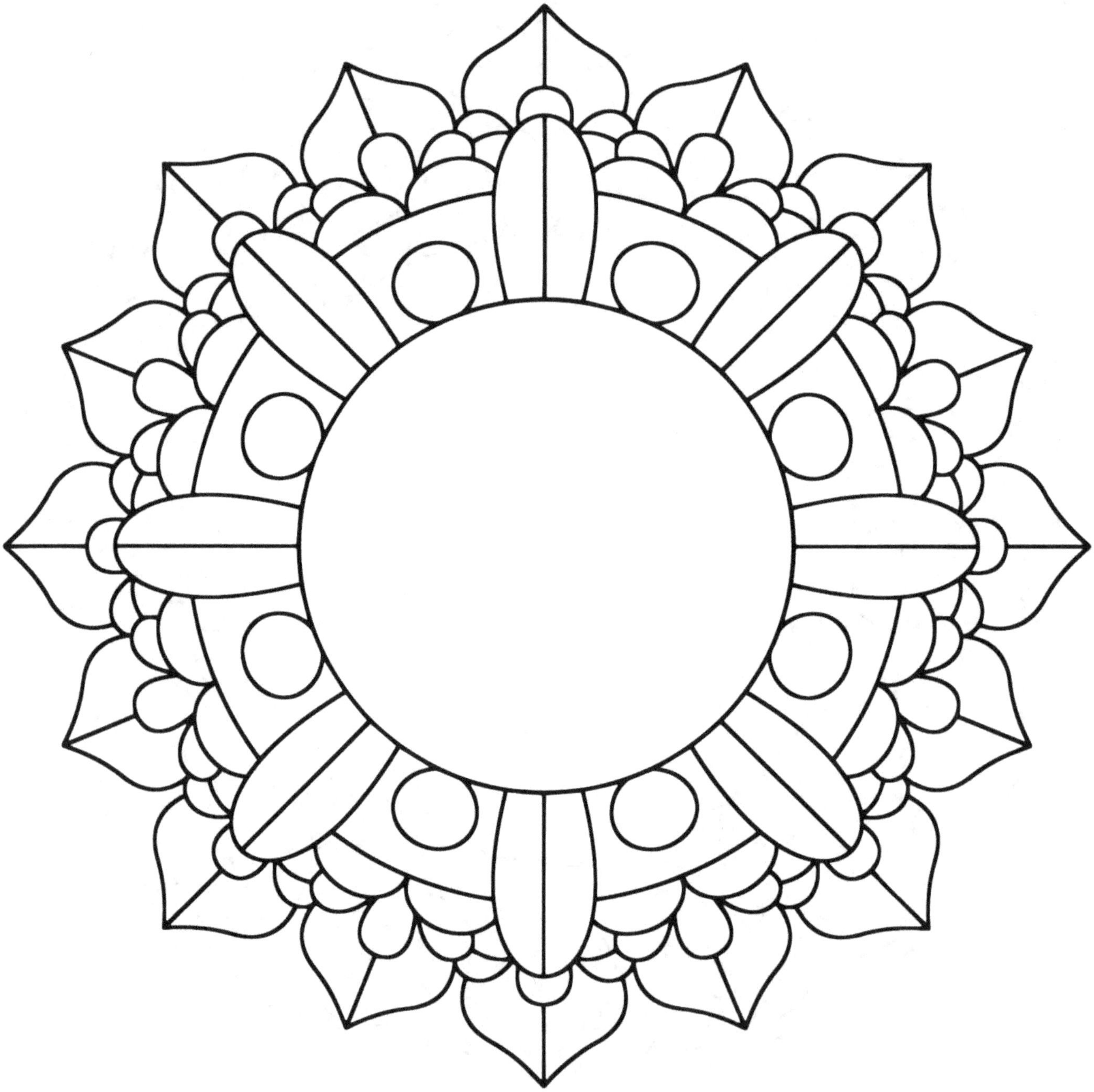

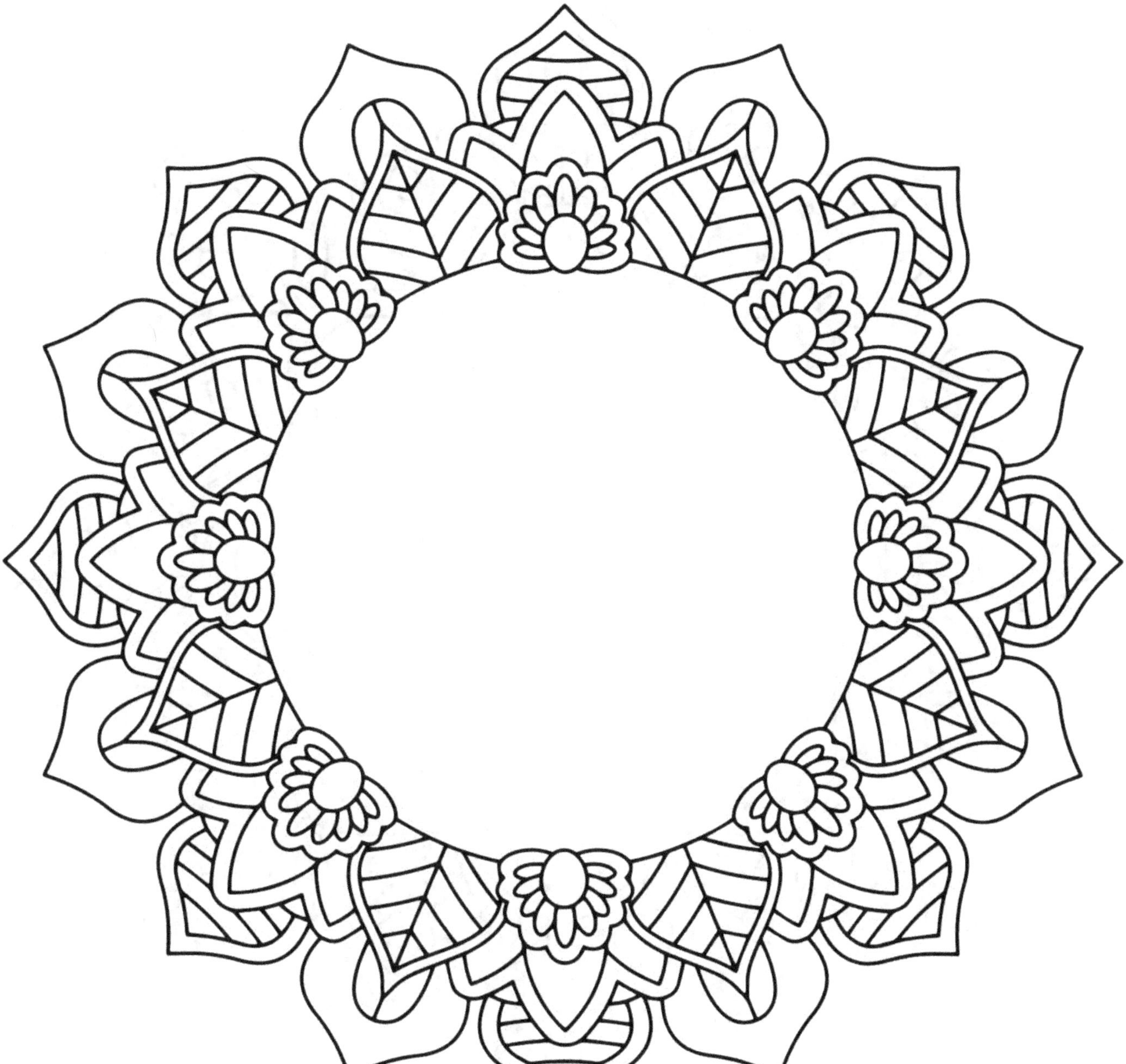

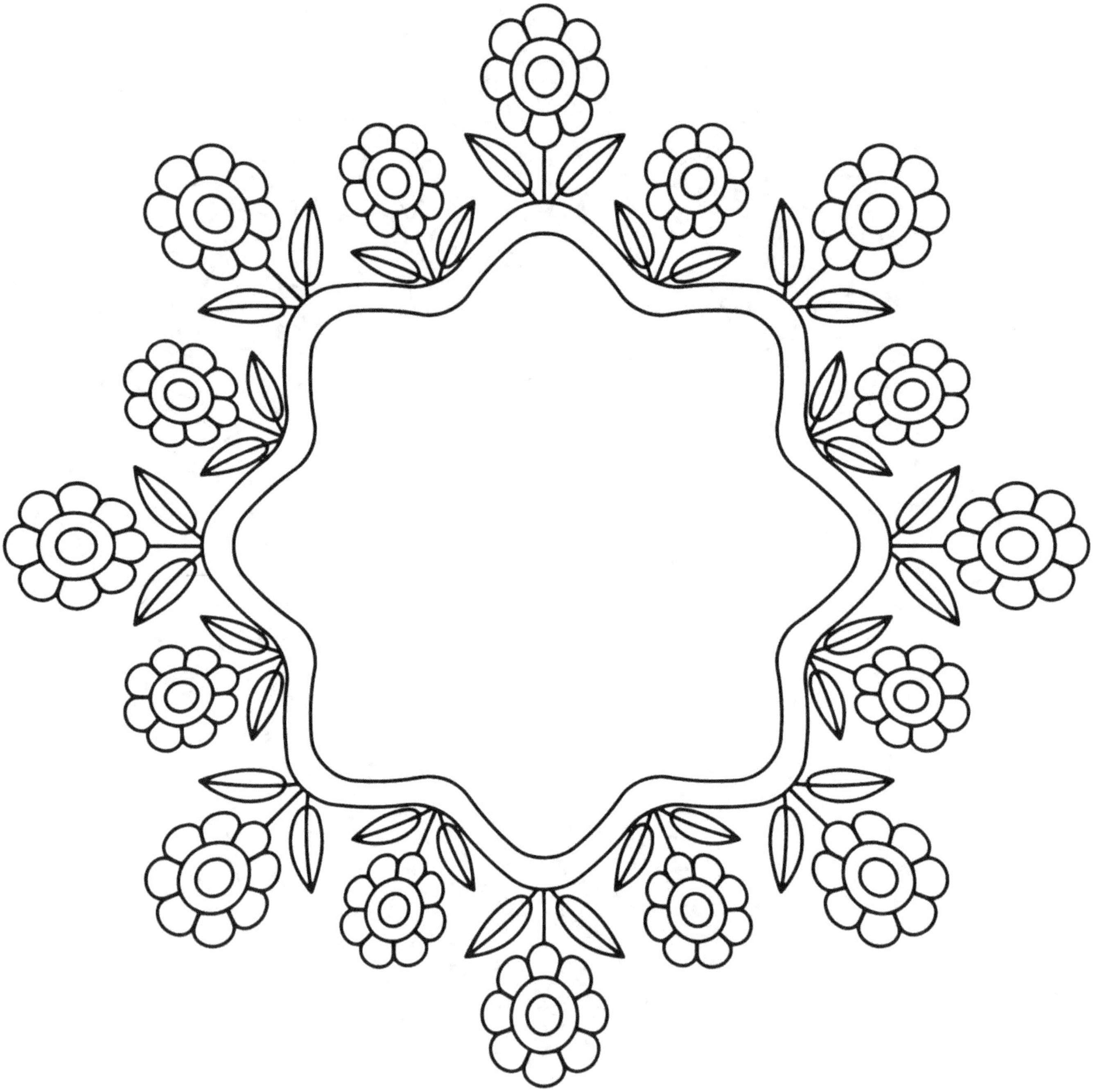

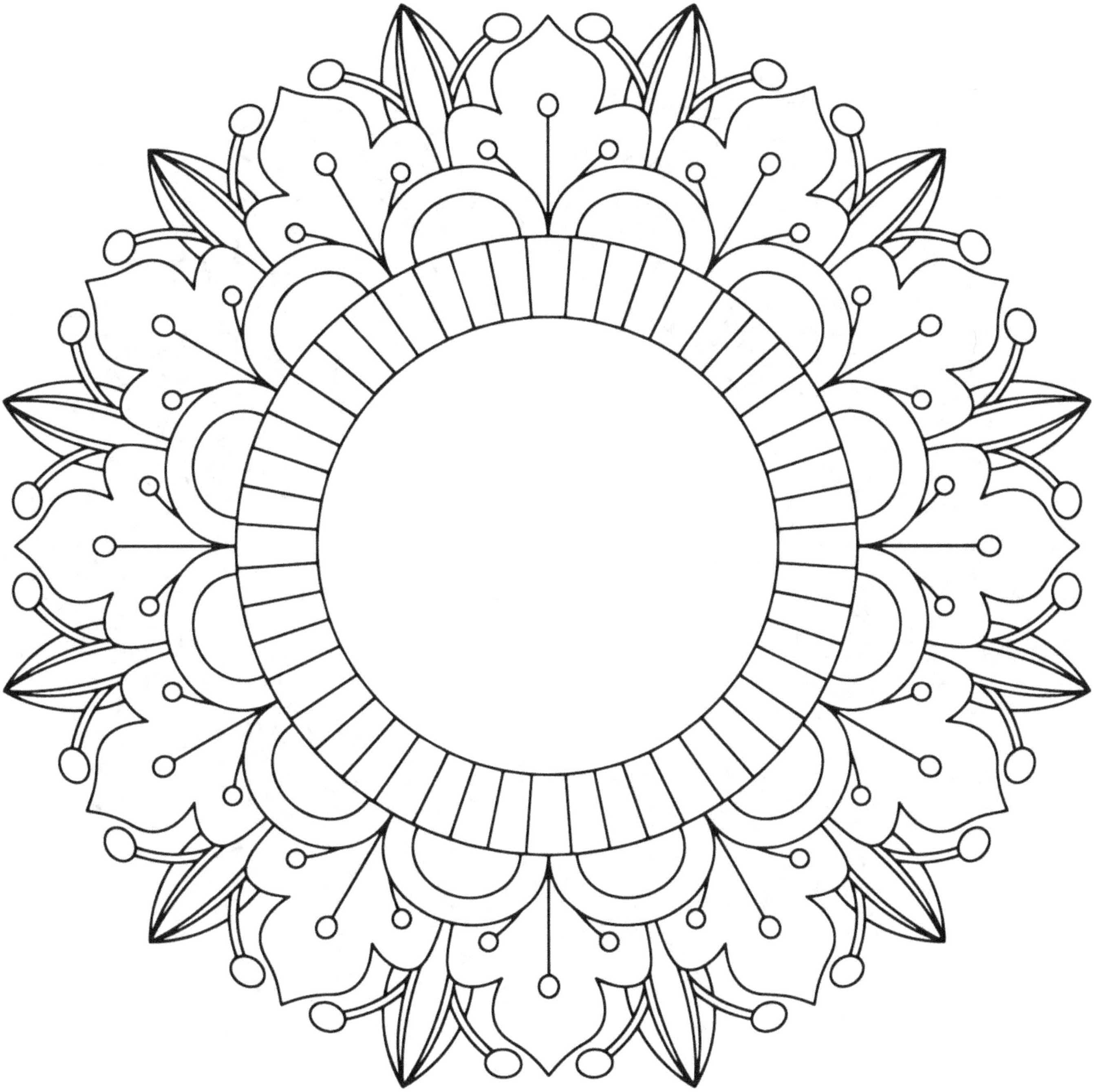

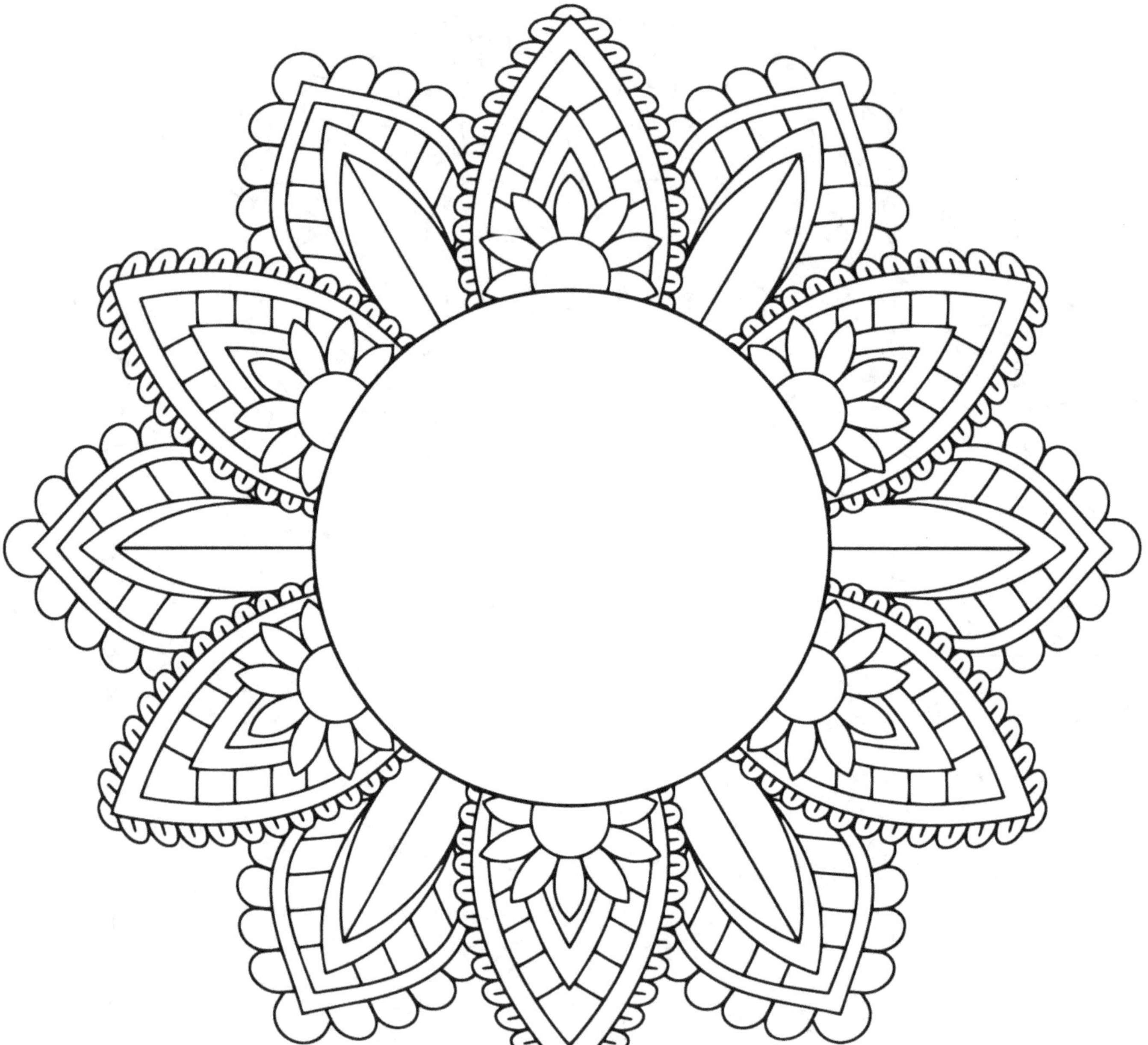

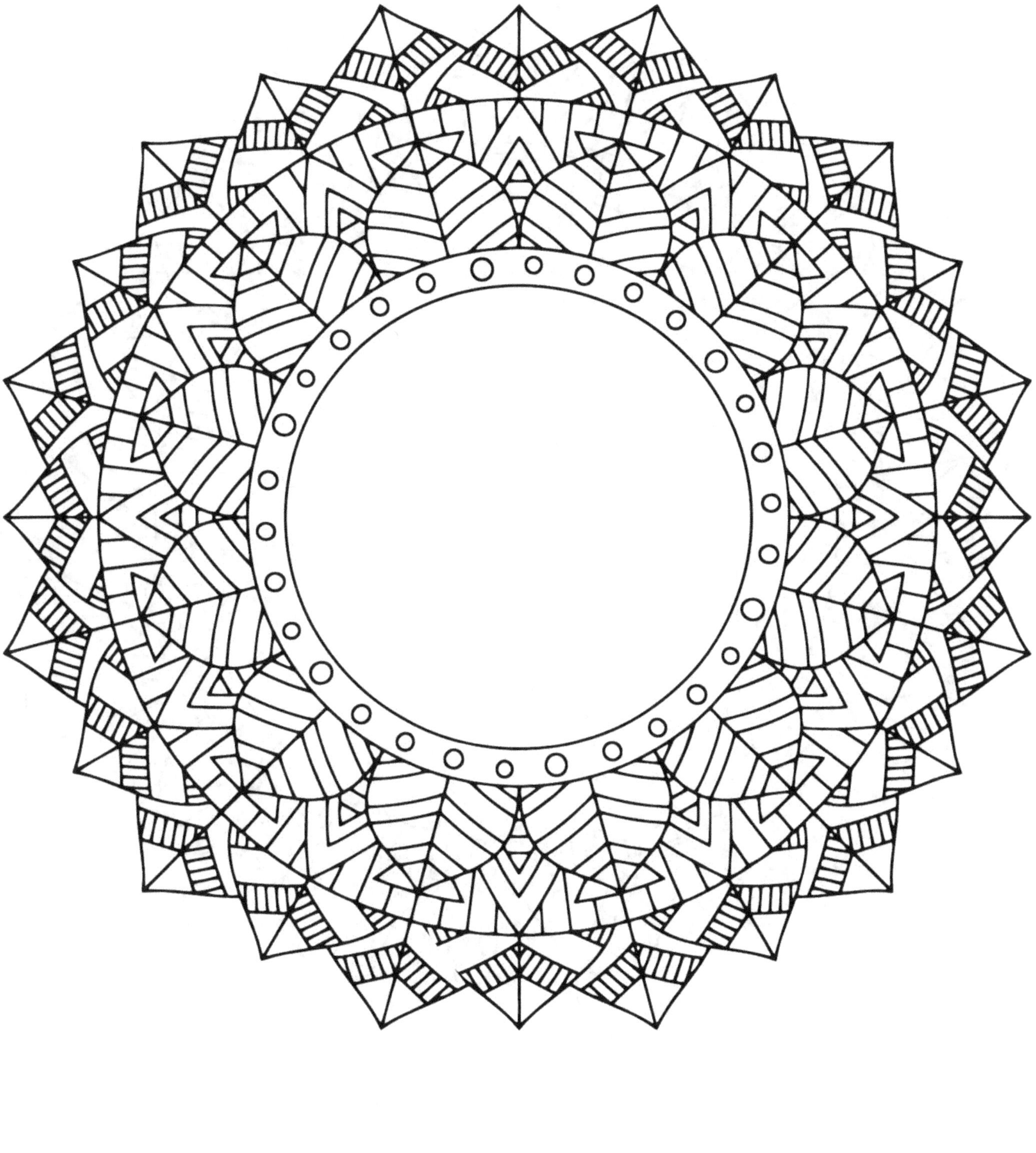

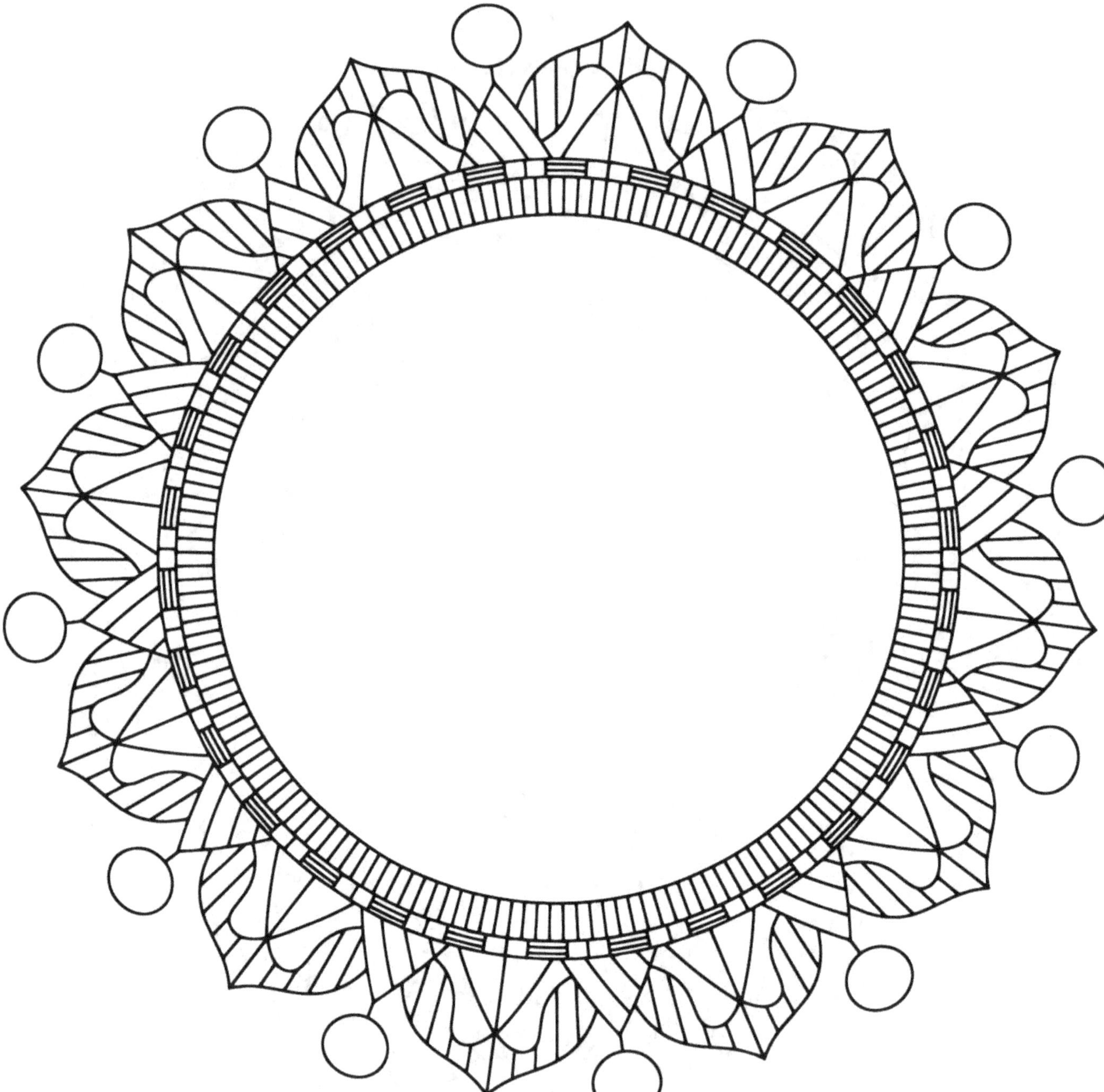

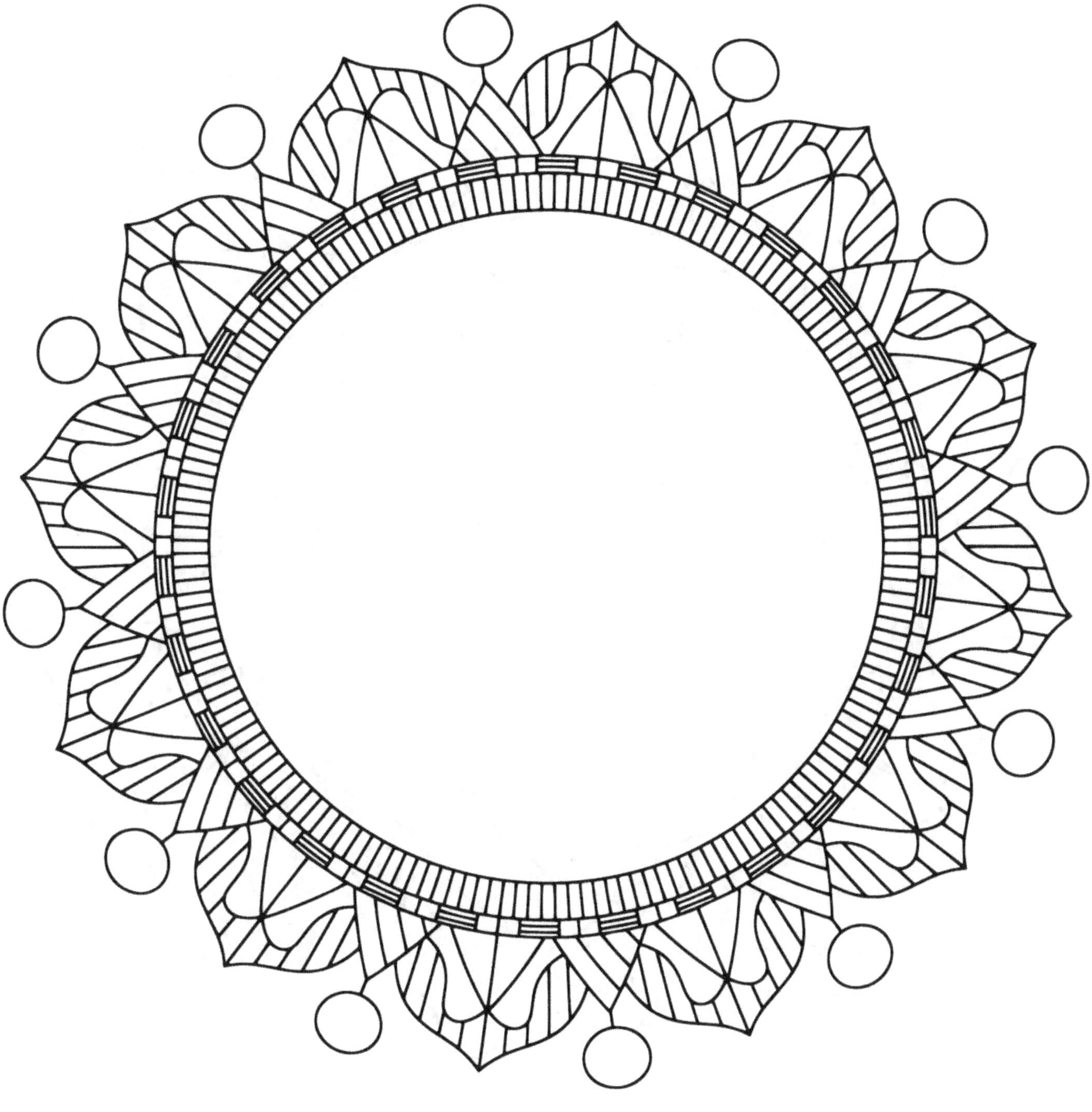

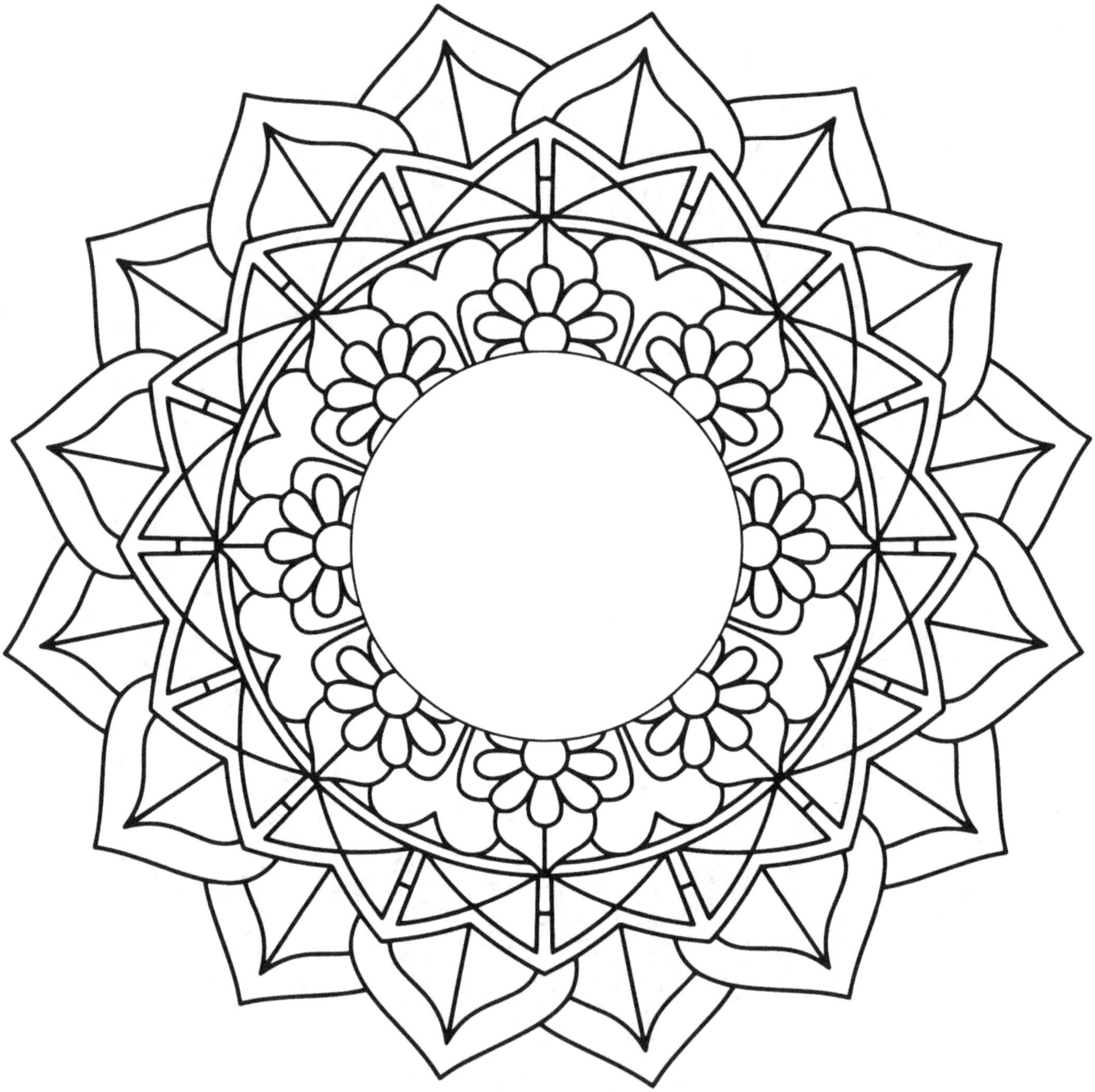

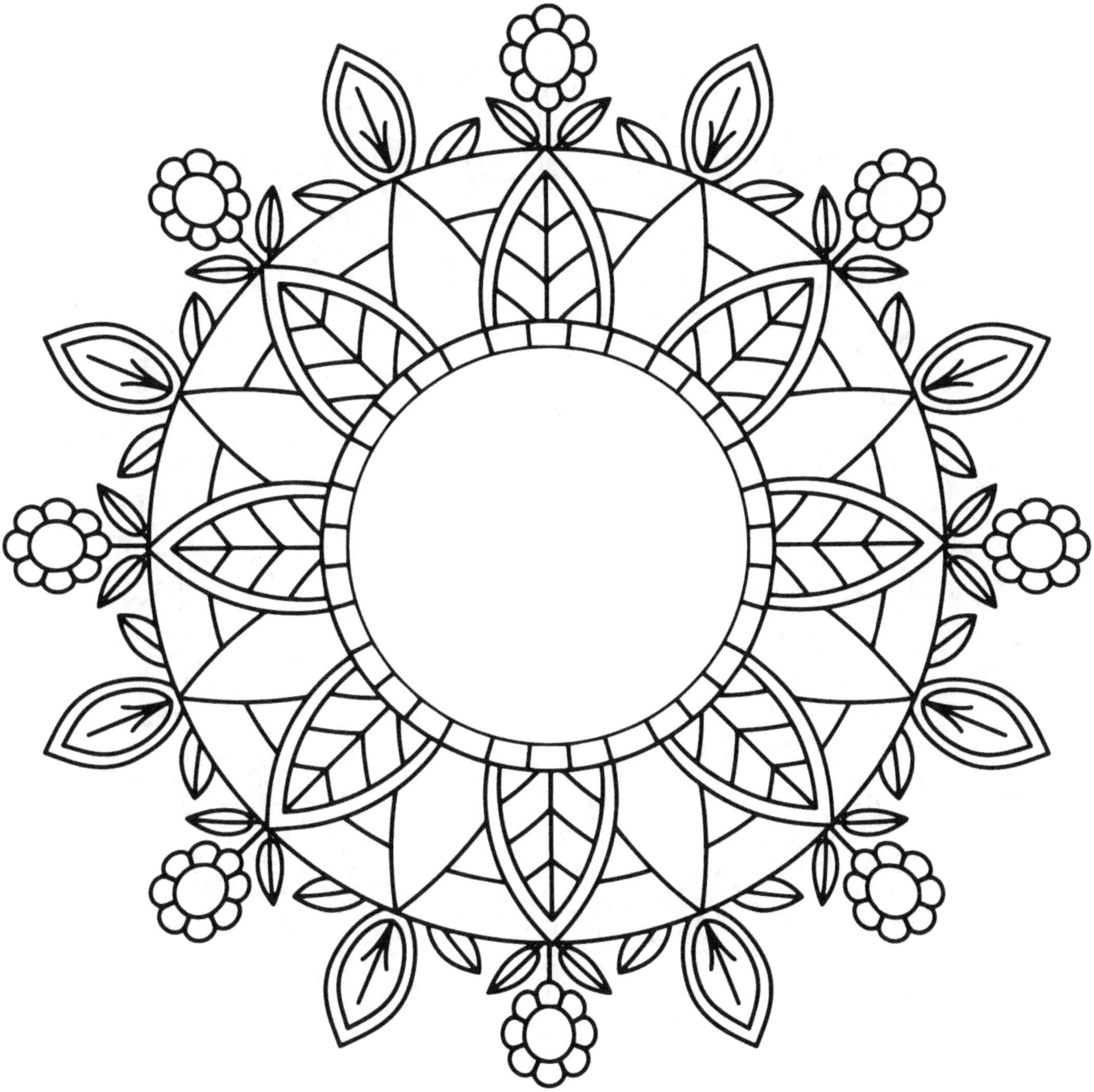

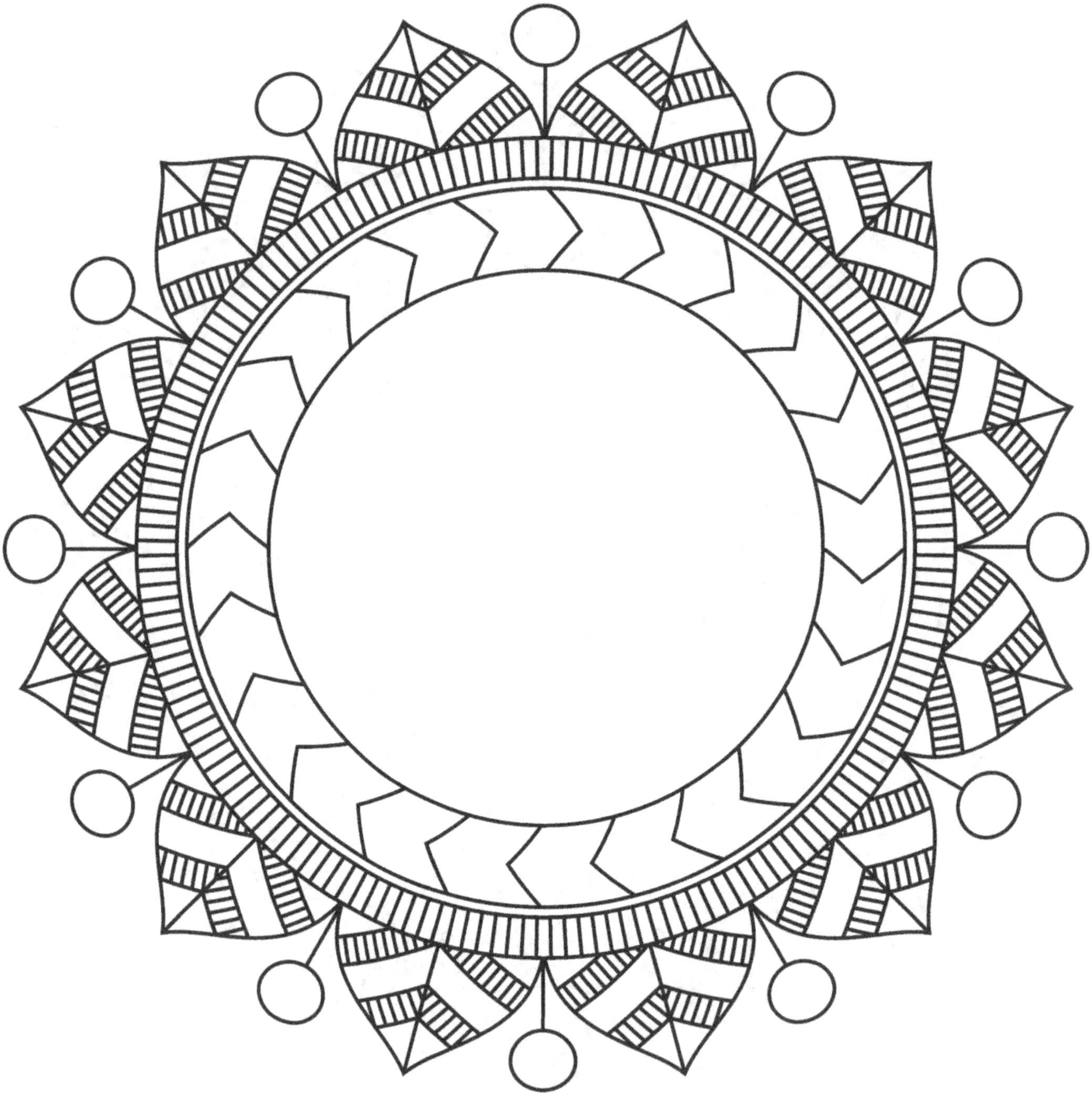

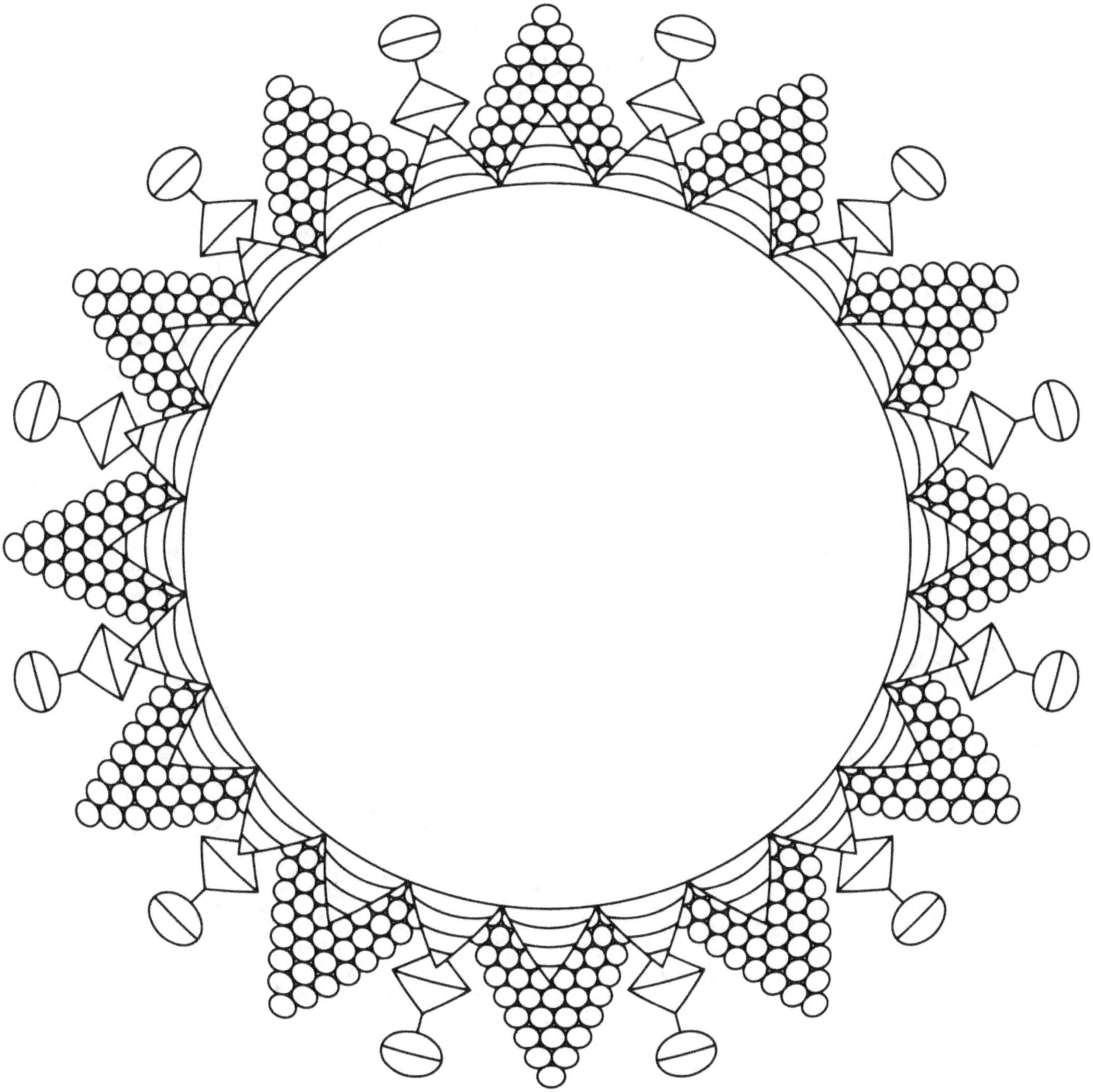

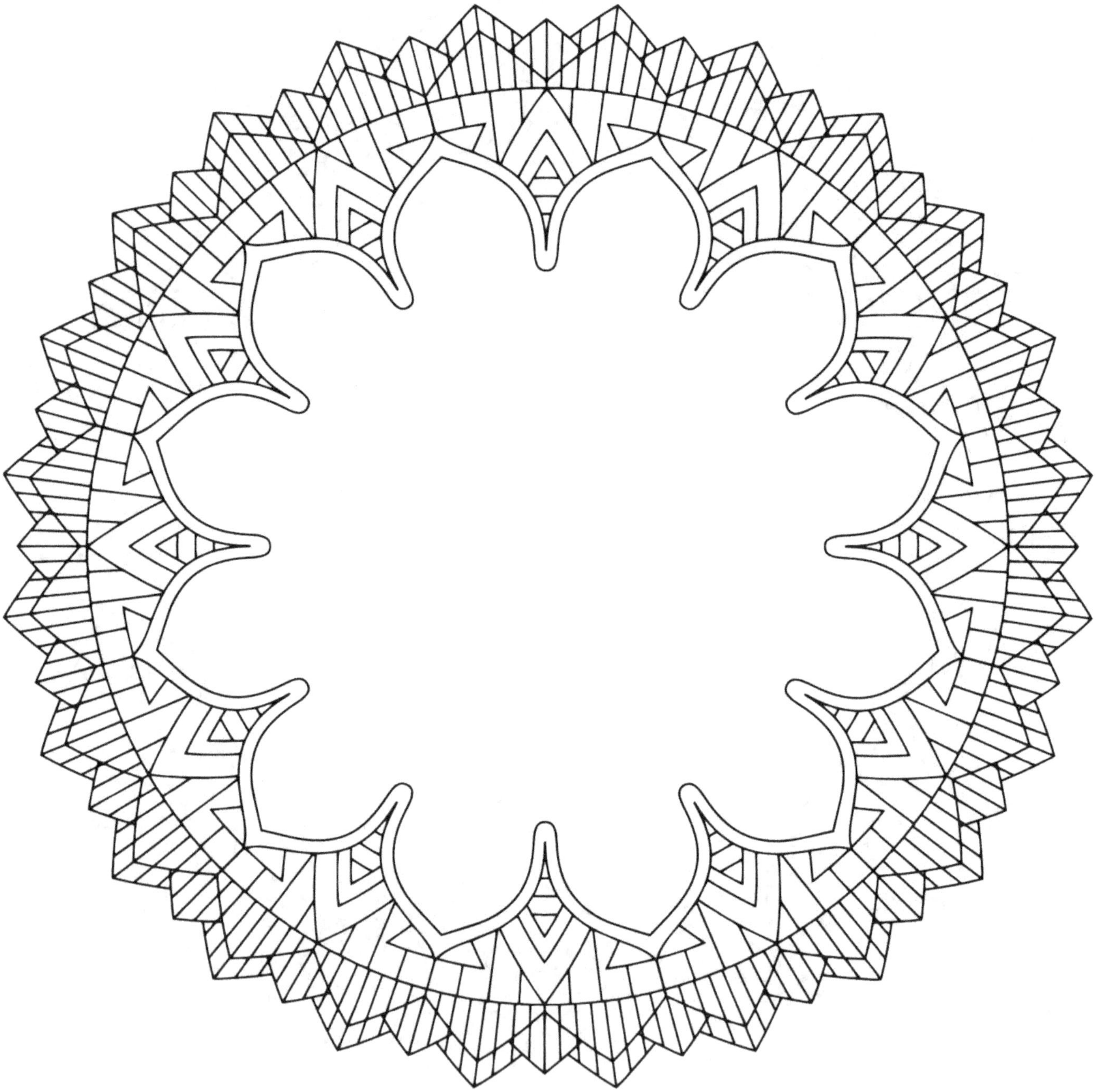

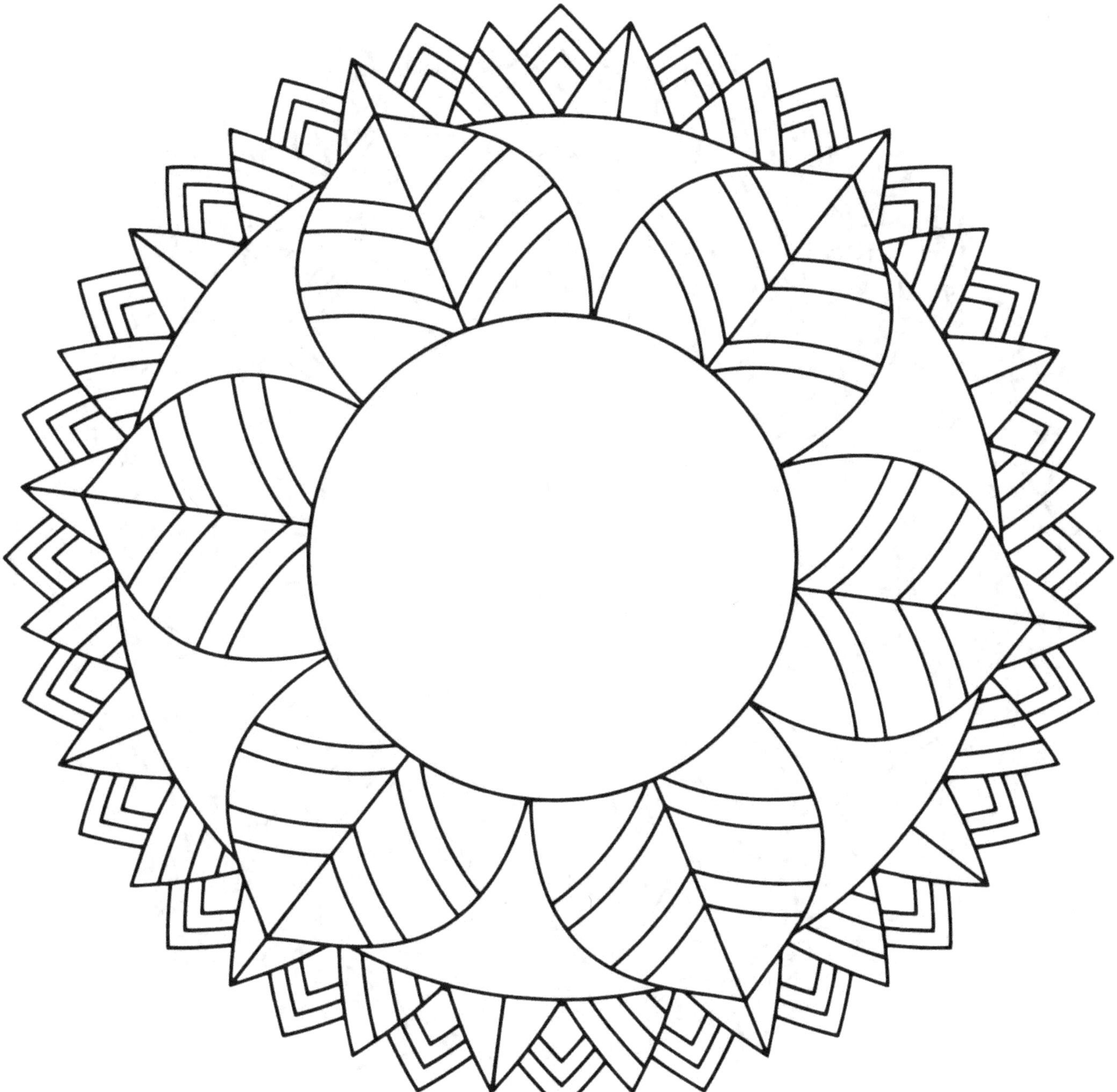

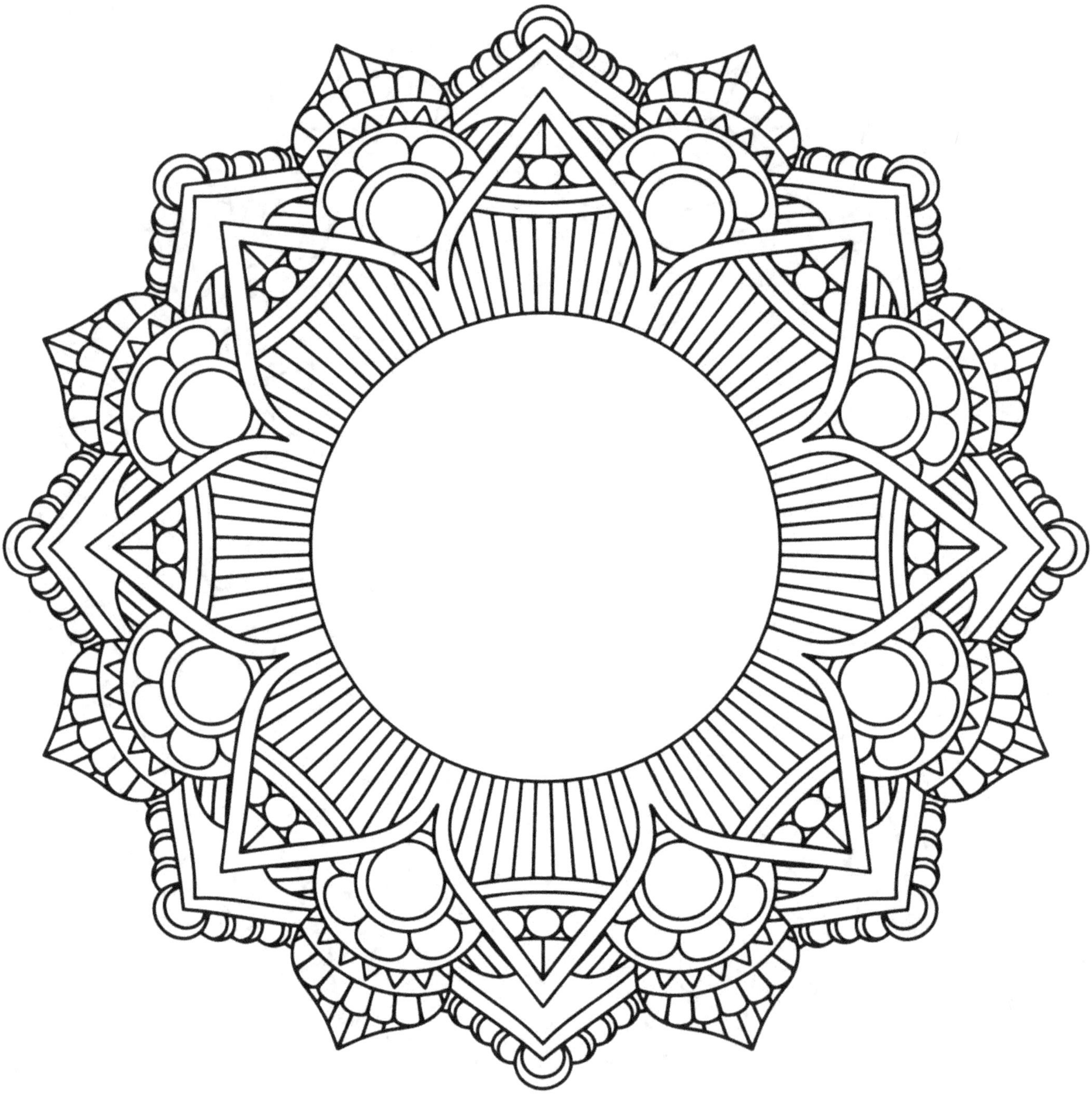

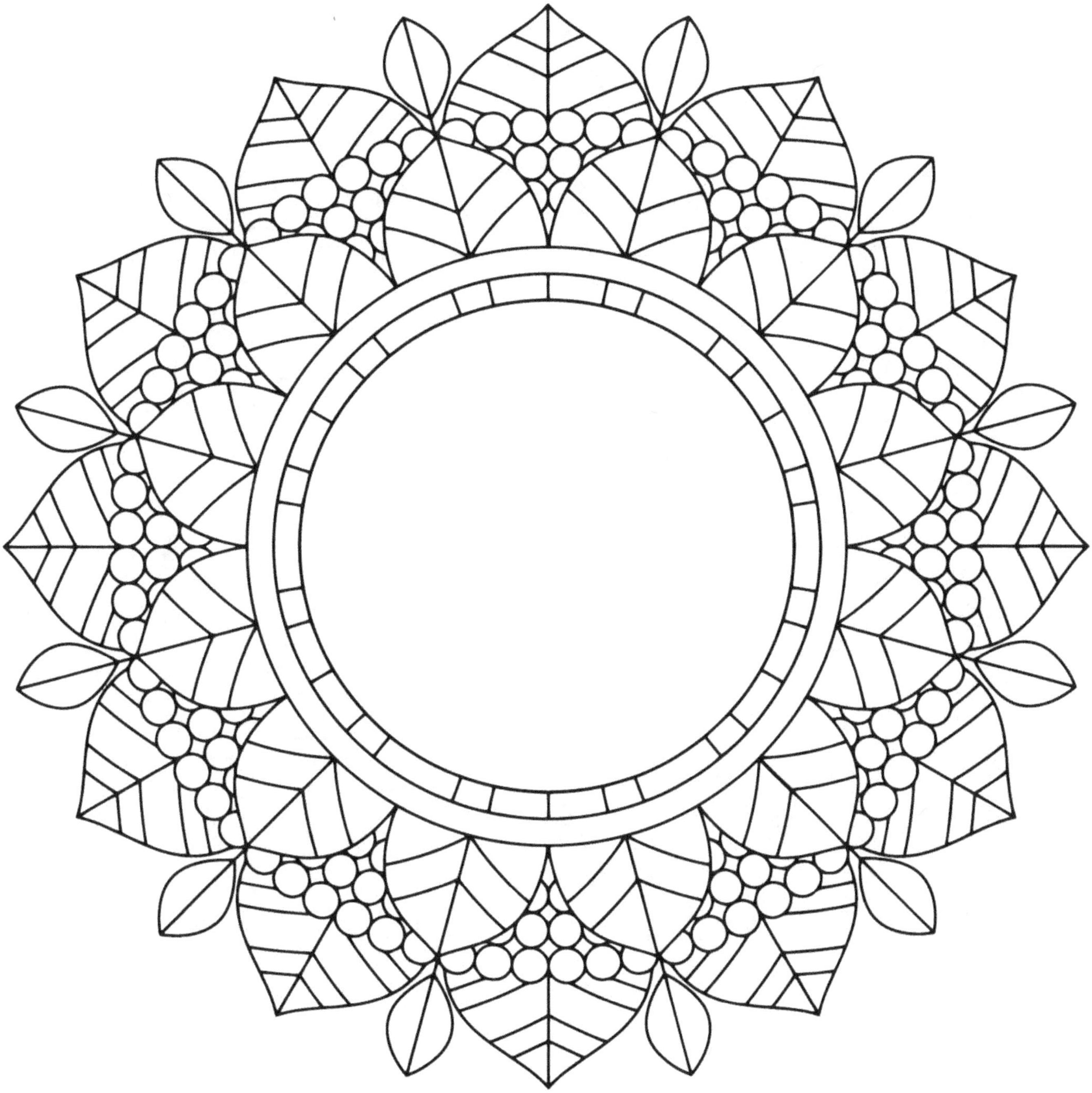

www.ingramcontent.com/pod-product-compliance
Lightning Source LLC
Chambersburg PA
CBHW080955220526
45465CB00008BA/3290

* 9 7 9 8 6 5 5 3 2 0 9 8 7 *